FORTY YEARS with The RIGHT WOMAN

A Memoir

Cecil Eugene Reinke

Order this book online at www.trafford.com
or email orders@trafford.com

Most Trafford titles are also available at major online book retailers.

Print information available on the last page.

ISBN: 978-1-4907-8731-2 (sc)
ISBN: 978-1-4907-8732-9 (hc)
ISBN: 978-1-4907-8737-4 (e)

Library of Congress Control Number: 2018934150

Trafford rev. 04/09/2018

 www.trafford.com
North America & international
toll-free: 1 888 232 4444 (USA & Canada)
fax: 812 355 4082

Author's Note

The drawing on the cover is by
Keryl Kris Reinke,
daughter of Cecil Eugene Reinke
and Carol Roehrich Reinke.

Dedication

To my wife, Carol Joyce Roehrich Reinke, who gave me a lifetime of joy and happiness; to my daughters, Keryl Kris Reinke and Alison Dale Reinke Smith, who enriched my life beyond imagination; to my granddaughters, Megan Leigh Smith, Emilee Anne Smith, and Rachel Nicole Smith, who embody the promising future of our American family; and to my niece, Norma Jean Rose Abercombie, a dedicated high school English teacher who provided invaluable assistance in the writing of this book.

Forty Years with The Right Woman

one

I saw her in the spring of my freshman year. I can still see her now.

The day was Monday, May 18, 1953. The occasion was a fraternity-sorority picnic, an evening get-together of about thirty guys from Sigma Alpha Epsilon and an equal number of girls from Kappa Alpha Theta. We were all students at North Dakota State University. The university is located in Fargo.

We were down on the banks of the Red River. The fest was well underway. We had a good fire going. Hot dogs were being cooked by the dozens and beer was flowing from kegs. Most of us were staying away from too much beer. Cokes and Pepsis were plentiful. But more than a few of my fraternity brothers were well on their way to becoming "snockered," with chug-a-lug challenges yet to come.

She was standing near the fire, surrounded by a dozen guys, all vying for attention. I was not part of the crowd. I was twenty feet away, and until it was almost time to pack up and return to the campus, I came no closer.

She was a radiant image, five feet two inches tall, less than ten pounds plus a hundred, perfectly arranged. She was wearing what I have ever since called her Woody Woodpecker jacket, a simple blue denim jacket with the cartoon character, seemingly half her size, stitched on the back. I saw shimmering brown hair, lightly peppered with strands of gold. The color in her eyes I could not see. I was blinded by the sparkle.

There was something about her, something very different. I remember thinking she was not the prettiest girl I ever saw, or even the prettiest girl at the picnic. Still, I found myself drawn to watching her. I was tempted to approach her, but I could not. The best I could do, shortly before we all went home, was walk close to her and say, "Nice night, isn't it." She smiled, "Yes, it's a beautiful evening."

She had dark brown eyes, shining of intelligence.

On the way back to the campus, I asked my brother Norman about her. Her name was Carol Roehrich. She was a sophomore. She lived in the women's dormitory.

When I got home from the picnic, I did something distinctly uncharacteristic of myself. I went to the phone and dialed the women's dormitory. Someone answered, and I asked to speak with Carol Roehrich. I waited nervously until she was on the line.

"Hello, Carol. This is Cecil Reinke. I'm one of the guys who were down at the river, one of the SAE's."

"Yes."

"Well, I was wondering --"

"Yes."

"Well, I was wondering if you would go to a movie or something with me, say next Friday night."

"I'm sorry, I can't."

"Oh well, I'm sorry, I just --

I was thinking I should get off the line, escape with dignity, when she interrupted. "Will you excuse me for a moment. Just stay on the line. I'll be right back."

Moments later, she was back. Days later, I learned that she had gone to ask if any of the girls in the dormitory knew anything about me. Among those asked were friends of my brother Norman, who suggested that I was likely a fairly decent fellow.

"Okay. Listen, I can't go because I have choir practice that night."

"I'm sorry."

"But if you like, you can meet me after."

"Fine, wonderful, I'll be there."

I was there that Friday night. I stood quietly in the rehearsal room listening to the choir sing. All I saw was she. I felt the same fascination I had during the picnic. Lucky me, I thought, looking forward to shared time with this girl.

We didn't have a lot of time. Girls were required to be in the dormitory by eleven. I took her to a little drive-in restaurant off campus, a place were they served something called a flying disk burger, a small sandwich made with two slices of bread, toasted and crimped along the edge. We talked in the car. I learned that she was born in Langdon, North Dakota, but now lived in Edgeley, where her father owned a small department store. I also learned that even though she was a sophomore and I was a freshman, she was a year younger. I liked her. I really liked her! Time up, I drove her back to the dormitory, and we said good night.

I have one story concerning our daughter Kris and flying disk burgers. Years later, while we were living in Galveston, Texas, I saw in a store a utensil that could be used to make something resembling a flying disk burger. Two steel bowls, facing each other, on long steel stems, perfectly sized to cook a hamburger patty between two slices of bread. I bought it, brought it home, and immediately made for my wife my version of a flying disk burger. I was obviously excited. Carol was amused but appreciative. Our daughter Kris, then about twelve, was curious. She asked her mother, "What's going on with Father?" Carol told her that, on our very first date, she and I had stopped for a flying disk. Kris was satisfied. "I knew it had to be something," she concluded. "Dad doesn't usually get this excited about kitchen equipment."

We had one more date the next week. Then school was out for the summer.

That summer I had a job painting Standard Oil trucks, or more accurately, as the assistant to a man hired to paint the trucks. The job paid each of us, painter and assistant, an hourly wage plus expenses for room and board. What we did was fairly simple. We washed the trucks, drove them to an open field, sprayed them with red paint, and applied decals reading "Standard Oil" on each side. Quick in, quick out, done! Well done?

This job was a real North Dakota geography lesson. We saw a significant number of the small towns in the state. One of the towns we came to was Edgeley, population 943. Edgeley, I knew very well, was where Carol Roehrich lived.

As Carol had told me, her father, Nicholas J. Roehrich, owned a department store on the main street. As an aside, Mr. Roehrich, like most German children of his age, and like my father, Christian Reinke, was at birth given only a first, no middle name. Somewhere in time, Nicholas Roehrich observed that most American men have both a first and middle name, plus of course their surname. He "remedied" the situation, assigning to himself the middle initial "J." I never heard him say what the "J" stood for, if name specific. My impression, always, was that he took an initial only. Notably, however, Carol's second oldest brother is named Nicholas James Roehrich, so likely, if the initial "J" stood for a specific name in Mr. Roehrich's mind, it stood for James.

Shortly after we arrived in Edgeley, I found a telephone and called Carol. "Will you be home this evening?" "Yes," she said. "May I come see you after work?" "Yes," she answered, inviting me to come to her home. She gave directions. Her home wasn't hard to find. As soon as my day's work was done, I cleaned up and rushed to see her.

At home with Carol were her parents, Nicholas and Grace Roehrich, and her little brother Ronnie. Her two older brothers, Bob and Jim, were away in the service, this being the time of the Korean War. Robert Dale Roehrich, her oldest brother, was in the Army, on the ground in Korea. Nicholas James Roehrich was in the Navy, on board a ship somewhere. I felt the same awkwardness as any young suitor meeting a girl's parents for the first time, although I knew they were trying to make me comfortable. I sensed a good, loving family atmosphere.

We visited for a little while. Then Carol invited me out for a drive in the family DeSoto. I remember little about the car, except that it had an automatic transmission. What I remember explicitly is watching Carol driving the car. It was the first time I had ever been in a car driven by a woman. We weren't out very long. It seemed wise to return early. Then it was goodbye, we'll see each other back at school.

There is one thing about this evening visit that I learned only years later, in fact, almost fifty years later. After Carol died, and after her father was gone, I visited with Carol's mother who was then in her nineties and living with Carol's brother Jim in Mesa, Arizona. We were sitting around their kitchen table talking. Mother Roehrich was remembering the first time she saw me, when I called Carol and visited with her family in Edgeley. "That night," she told me, "I turned to Nick and said, 'This is the one. That's the boy Carol is going to marry.'"

two

One of the most pleasant memories of my life is of a train trip from Clinton, Oklahoma, to Fargo, North Dakota. The year was 1952. The month was September.

I was traveling with my brother Norman. I had graduated from Clinton High School the previous spring and worked that summer driving a truck in the wheat harvest. My brother Norman was recently out of the Army. We were on our way to college, to attend North Dakota State University. The train was filled with college students, good guys and wonderful girls. We gathered in the dining car, talked, horsed around, played cards, and enjoyed each other's company. Our hearts were filled with the spirit of adventure.

For those too young to easily visualize the year 1952, a few notes may help.

Harry Truman was in his last months as President of the United States. Dwight David Eisenhower and Adlai E. Stevenson were campaigning to succeed him.

World War II had ended seven years earlier, followed by "Cold War."

Six months earlier, on February 15, 1952, King George VI died. Elizabeth II acceded to the British throne and was proclaimed head of the British Commonwealth.

In November, 1952, Eisenhower was elected President of the United States.

That same November, John F. Kennedy was elected to the U. S. Senate.

One year earlier, on May 12, 1951, the United States tested a hydrogen bomb.

Two years earlier, on June 25, 1950, North Korea invaded South Korea. On June 30, President Truman, in league with the United Nations, authorized the use of American forces to repel the invasion. This "Hot War" was called a "Police Action." As asserted by the President, "The United States is not at war." We were actively "not at war" in Korea for more than three years. When the shooting stopped, on July 28, 1953, almost 25,000 American military personnel had been killed. Over 100,000 Americans were injured.

While on this train to Fargo, Norman and I were not thinking about bombs, or elections, or coronations, or war. We were having fun. We were headed for college.

I say we were on our way to attend North Dakota State University. Actually, on the day we made this trip and for all the days of our attendance, the school was named the North Dakota Agricultural College. We respectfully referred to the college as "N. D. A. C.," or "the A. C.," or just plain "Old Ma." Years later the name was changed to "North Dakota State University." If I said we were headed for the North Dakota Agricultural College only a few old timers would know what school I was talking about. For this reason, I take license and refer to our school by its current name, North Dakota State University, or as is more commonly said, North Dakota State.

Why were we going to North Dakota State?

The short answer is that Norman wanted us to go to school in Fargo. The longer answer is that our father, Christian Reinke, our sister Edna, and our brother Walter were in

North Dakota. Our sister Edna lived in Fargo. Our brother Walter lived in Cooperstown. Our father stayed sometimes with Edna, sometimes with Walter. The ultimate answer is that our family had a long association with the State of North Dakota. Our paternal great-grandparents, Andreas and Louisa Reinke, immigrated to the United States from Russia in 1885 and homesteaded in North Dakota. They were accompanied by their son Daniel and his wife Juliana, our paternal grandparents, who homesteaded in North Dakota. Our maternal grandparents, Johann Gottfried and Eva Schulz, migrated from Russia in 1898 and settled in North Dakota. They brought to America their three year old daughter Fredericka, the small girl who would one day blossom into our mother. Our father was born in North Dakota. Our parents were married in North Dakota. Our two oldest brothers, John and Emil, and our four sisters, Lydia, Edna, Alice, and Ruth, were born in North Dakota. Not until 1924 did our family move to Oklahoma. Only our parent's four youngest children, Walter, Ruben, Norman and I, were born in Oklahoma.

Our mother died in Clinton, Oklahoma, when I was two years old, Norman four. Fredericka Schulz Reinke was born in Russia, Klaystitz, Bessarabia, on September 15, 1895. She died on August 8, 1935. She was thirty-nine years, ten months, and twenty-three days old.

I don't really remember my mother, although I know a lot about her. I know how very much she loved me.

My brother Walter told me how our father slumped home from the Western Oklahoma Baptist Hospital on the day she died, looking like he had lost his whole world.

I am often asked by friends in Oklahoma why I went to college in North Dakota. I like to tell them in jest, "Well, it's like this. I had been to North Dakota often, always in the summer, working on our family farm. Nobody ever told me it got cold in the winter."

Getting into college was a different experience in 1952 than it is today. Now, students apply for colleges at least a year in advance. They send applications to numerous colleges, complete with high school grade records and personal activity descriptions; then they run to mail boxes hoping to have been accepted, too often disappointed. Norman and I were depression babies, born in 1931 and 1933 respectively, years that produced few American children. For us, colleges were not crowded. We could have been heading for any university in America with confidence that we would be accepted. Our experience, in light of what is required today, seems unbelievable. When we got to Fargo, we found the campus of North Dakota State, walked into the Registrar's office and announced that we wanted to attend. Norman had earlier completed one year of college at Oklahoma City University before entering the Army, but he had with him no records. I told them I was a high school graduate, albeit without either my diploma or a copy of my high school transcript. These omissions of documentation didn't seem to bother the people in the Registrar's office. They simply gave us admission applications, had us fill them out, and sent us to another building on the campus to take a battery of tests. They would send for our records. We were in!

One of the things I was asked when we registered was what I wanted to study. Clinton High School had done very little by way of educating my class on available vocations. Other than teaching, I knew of only three professions, law, medicine and engineering. I chose law, and on my application entered pre-law as what I wanted. They say ignorance is bliss. For me, this proved to be true. Following three years of pre-law at North Dakota State, I was in law school at the University of North Dakota, located in Grand Forks. From day one I loved the law. To me, it is the most honorable profession on earth. Of course, I went to law school when professors were still emphasizing that the purpose of our profession is to protect widows, orphans, and children. I was taught that lawyers were to represent the positions of their clients, not views, opinions, and causes of their own.

three

During our first year at North Dakota State the school had no student union. Adjacent to the campus, however, was a small restaurant called the Hasty-Tasty. Norman was a coffee drinker. I had not yet learned to drink coffee, but I tried, seeking palatability in excesses of cream and sugar. Between classes we would gather with other students at the Hasty-Tasty for discussions, drinks, snacks, or an occasional run at the pinball machine. It was a cherished little haven. Norman was particularly good then, as he has been all his life, at getting to know people. So very shortly we knew a great many students on campus, and they knew us. Being from Oklahoma, we stood out. To the ears of newly made friends, we had what were decidedly "Sooner" accents.

North Dakota State had a substantial number of fraternities and sororities. Candidly, in today's world of larger universities, where fraternities and sororities abide exclusionists, were I a college president, I would want to bar them from campus. But North Dakota State was a small school, enrollment fewer than three thousand. Our fraternities and sororities were not creators of crushed egos. Anyone who wanted to join a fraternity or sorority was welcomed. Norman and I were approached by members of a number of fraternities. Norman could join none of them because while attending Oklahoma City University he had pledged and become a member of Lambda Chi Alpha. Had Lambda Chi had a presence at North Dakota State, I would have joined the fraternity of my brother, but it did not. Because I best liked what I saw in its members, I joined Sigma Alpha Epsilon. Norman, while not a member of Sigma Alpha Epsilon, might just as well have been. He was given full access to all facilities and expected to attend all fraternity functions. In fact, he did everything but attend our "secret" meetings.

North Dakota State is a land grant college. Except for veterans, all male students were required to enroll in the Reserve Officers Training Corps, ROTC. Each student had a choice to join either the Army ROTC or the Air Force ROTC. I was the youngest of ten children, of six brothers. My oldest brother John and second oldest brother Emil had served in World War II, in the Army. My brother Walter, third, was in the Navy during World War II. My brother Ruben, at this time, was in the Army, somewhere in Korea. Norman was just out of the Army. Less than two months earlier, he had been attending Officers Candidate School at Fort Knox, Kentucky. A barrage of guns fired from tanks damaged his ears. No longer able to hear well enough to serve, he was released early from the Army. Had North Dakota State had a Navy ROTC program, I likely would have joined that because my brother Walter, the sailor, was always for me a role model. But my choice was between the Army and the Air Force. Given my family history, I belonged in the Army. I joined the Army ROTC.

Norman received a small monthly check from the Government, support from the GI Bill of Rights, which he shared with me. Still, we both had to work in order to stay in school. I think we were of the last generation for which tuition and other expenses were sufficiently low that a student actually could "work his or her way through college."

I got a job working for Swanston Nash, an automobile dealership in Fargo. I was, put most kindly, a flunky. Sometimes I would wash cars. But mostly I ran around in a company Jeep, delivering or picking up parts for mechanical repairs. One of the jobs I found most interesting was picking up estimates for our body shop. In those days, insurance companies required three estimates before they would authorize repairs. Whenever someone brought a wrecked car to our dealership for repairs, our body shop foreman would prepare an estimate. He would give his estimate to me and tell me where to go to get two other estimates. I would drive to the designated repair shops and show our estimate to whoever was in charge and come back with a second and third estimate, always higher.

It was while working for Swanston Nash that I learned to drink coffee. One of my jobs was to make coffee for the mechanics. It needed to be ready by two-thirty each afternoon, which was when they took their break. I made the coffee in a large, white enamel pot, with no insides. I boiled the water, threw in the grounds, and let them cook. All of the men took their coffee straight, presumably of necessity since I never saw any cream or sugar. Once the mechanics arrived, I had a choice. I could sit and drink coffee with the men, or I could go back to work. I learned to drink it black, no sugar.

Swanston Nash was a good place for me to work. The pay was generous for the type of work involved. I was paid more than the other flunkies, I believe because I was a college student. Billy Swanston, the son of Mr. Swanston, the owner, was a graduate of North Dakota State. He was then about thirty years of age. I think he liked the idea of sponsoring a student. The Swanstons were also generous to me in ways not measured in money. On several occasions, for significant social events at the school such as the Charity Ball and the Military Ball, I was provided the use of a brand new Nash.

Norman and I needed a car. We lived off campus, because it was less expensive. I spoke to Billy Swanston. He found us a used vehicle in excellent shape, which he sold to us cheap. It was a 1946 Plymouth coupe, the model with a small back seat. One thing about this car is particularly memorable. It had no switch for the windshield wipers, only two little prongs sticking up where the knob was missing. I suppose we could have bought a knob, but we never did. We found that if you stuck a dime between the prongs you could turn on the wipers. Actually, our little Plymouth became somewhat famous on campus because everyone was soon aware of the presence of the dime.

I have a story involving Billy Swanston that I like to tell, and he would forgive me. I was pretty much standing around while a fellow flunky, not a college student, likely a high school dropout, was busy washing a car. Billy walked up to him and said, "That's how I got started, at the bottom of the ladder." The young man, probably no more than sixteen, put down his wash cloth and responded, "Yes sir, Mr. Swanston, that's true. But you must remember your daddy owned the ladder."

Another story I like to tell concerning Billy Swanston, one he would likely enjoy my telling, involves his dating practices while a student at North Dakota State. Billy had a reputation for calling late, and calling one girl after another down a list until he hit acceptance. On one occasion he telephoned a girl I will call Betty. This girl declined his invitation. "Sorry Billy," she chided, "no can do. Better keep going down your list." To this Billy

Swanston reportedly replied, "I can't, Betty. This is the bottom."

While a freshman at North Dakota State, I suffered the first and worst drunkenness experience of my life. I was sitting in the fraternity house, visiting with a fellow pledge, Guy Enabnit, when Thomas Peckscamp came looking for someone to go out drinking with him. Tommy was a member of our fraternity who had graduated the year before. He was a lieutenant in the Air Force, home on furlough. I had never drunk any hard liquor and had tasted very little beer. I was from Oklahoma, a dry state. Of course, Oklahoma had numerous bootleggers, and the sophisticated guys knew how to buy booze. But I was not one of them. Anyway, there we were, Guy and I, nobody else in the house. If an alumnus home from the Air Force wanted someone to accompany him on a spree, it was thought to be our duty to go.

We started with the bars in Fargo. I was drinking screwdrivers, orange juice and vodka. You couldn't taste the liquor. Tommy and Guy were drinking whatever they were drinking. At twelve o'clock the bars in Fargo closed. We did not go home. Instead, we went across the Red River to Moorhead, Minnesota. There the bars wouldn't close until one o'clock in the morning. One o'clock came, and still we didn't go home. Rather, Tommy took us to his house. When we arrived at the Peckscamp home, Mr. Peckscamp got up. Proud of his boy home from the service, Mr. Peckscamp wanted to fix us something to drink. He chose coffee royals, black coffee with a touch of bourbon. We were drinking, and singing old fraternity songs. At times, either I or Guy or both of us didn't know all the words. If we weren't singing loud enough, Mr. Peckscamp assumed that we had not had enough to drink. Splash! Into the coffee, more bourbon.

What time Tommy finally brought us back to the fraternity house I don't know. How Guy made out I don't know; I never asked. What I do know is that I suffered on the living room couch, unable to move, for what seems like three days. Something else I know. Fifty-some years of days and nights have come and gone. I have never since even sipped on a screwdriver or sniffed a coffee royal.

four

It is possible that someone, somewhere, enjoyed going to college as much as I did, but I doubt it. My first year at North Dakota State was great. The second and third years were even better. I had, as they say, the time of my life.

During my second year, Norm and I were joined by our brother Ruben. Just out of the Army, after service in Korea, Ruben was twenty-four years old when he registered as a freshman. He was welcomed into the fraternity I belonged to, Sigma Alpha Epsilon. He was a joy to me, to Norman, and to the whole student body.

Carol and I dated regularly, but not exclusively. From time to time I went out with other girls, and often I had fun. She had several serious suitors, honorable guys that I knew well.

She was selective about which invitations for dates she would accept. Once she received a call from one of the guys on campus in whom she definitely had no interest. She had read an article advising that when a girl receives a call from someone that she knows she would never want to date, the proper thing for her to do is to tell that person that she was not interested and to ask that he not call again. On this occasion she decided to follow the writer's advice.

"I'm really not interested," she told the guy. "Please don't call me again."

"Well," he told her, "don't think you're so smart Carol Roehrich. I already called four girls before you."

Funny? Yes. But Carol did not think so. She had not intended hurt feelings.

Carol did go with me to most of the more significant social events on campus.

One evening while we were together attending the Charity Ball, Carol and I were outside walking on a beautifully manicured lawn, each carrying an alcoholic drink of some kind. She looked at her glass and asked me, "Cecil, would it be a waste if I poured this out?" Drawing on wisdom I didn't know I possessed, I answered, "No more of a waste than if you drank it."

Carol worked on the student newspaper, the Spectrum, and on our college yearbook, the Bison. I served a football season as sports editor of the Spectrum.

Carol delighted in telling me about her little brother Ronnie. One time when he was around eight years old, he came home from a visit to the stockyards. "Do you know how pigs are born?" he asked her. "Yes I do," she answered. "Oh, no you don't," he insisted. Another time she saw him in deep thought. She asked him what he was thinking about. "Well, it's puzzling," he answered. "How do drakes do it?"

At the time Ronnie was born, Carol was seven years old. Her new little brother was not a beautiful baby, she would admit. He was ruddy and wrinkled, but it didn't matter. She loved him, her love liken to that of a mother. She delighted in believing that by the time he was two years old her little brother was the cutest kid in town.

One day a neighbor lady was visiting in the Roehrich home. "My, your little brother is a cute boy," the woman said to Carol. "Yes he is," Carol was quick to agree. Later, Grace Roehrich told her daughter that when someone compliments her little brother she should just say "Thank you." "I don't see why," Carol rejoined. "He is cute."

During my second year in college, her third, Carol asked me what I thought of her little brother. My answer was not the best I have ever given. I said, "He's an ordinary kid." She was not impressed with my judgment. A cold wind encircled our courtship.

I gained an interesting insight into the way Carol thought about life and family on a day we were having coffee in the student union. Recall that when Norman and I first arrived at North Dakota State, the campus had no student union. We used the Hasty-Tasty. The student union was under construction during our second year and opened at the beginning of our third. Carol never came to the Hasty-Tasty, but she loved the new student union. We were sitting at a large booth with a group of students when Ray Harchanko, a fraternity brother of mine, said to her, "Carol, you don't appreciate a thing you have." Unlike Ruben, Norman, and me, and Ray, Carol did not have to work while in college. Nicholas J. and Grace Roehrich saw to everything their daughter needed. Carol's parents, she well knew, had started with nothing and worked very hard to support their children, especially during the depression years. Carol was sitting in the booth, extremely well dressed and wearing a fur coat. She looked at Ray Harchanko and said, "You're right, I don't appreciate a thing I have. But I appreciate why I have it."

While Norman and I were in our third year at the college, Ruben in his second, our father died. Christian Reinke died in Cooperstown, North Dakota, on Thursday, March 10, 1955. He was four days short of being sixty five years old. He was born on the family farm near Klum, North Dakota, on March 14, 1890. Funeral services were held in Litchville, North Dakota. Carol and her parents came to his funeral although only Carol, neither of her parents, actually knew my dad. Nicholas J. and Grace attended out of respect for their daughter's wishes. All ten of father's children and most of his grandchildren were present. Father's six sons—John, Emil, Walter, Ruben, Norman and I—were pallbearers.

We had known for more than a year that our father was terminally ill. The summer before he died, the entire Reinke clan got together for a reunion in Cooperstown, North Dakota. We all gathered to honor this honorable man.

Dad's first-born child and oldest son John Emanuel with his wife "Doll," Dolores Melinda, and their three children, daughter Melinda Dolores and sons Joseph John and Edward John, came from New Jersey. His first daughter and second oldest child Lydia Pauline, with her husband Ray Sanders and daughters Mildred LaVonne and Rae Lynne; his second son Emil Arthur with his wife Treva and son Danny Chris; and his third daughter Alice Alora with her husband Bundy Rose and her first three children, daughters Norma Jean, Barbara Ann, and Linda Diane, drove up from Oklahoma. His fourth and youngest daughter Ruth Eva, with her husband Thomas Ciliberto, daughter Margaret Christine and son Thomas, Jr., came from Rhode Island. His second daughter Edna Amelia, a widow, and her children Bobbie Jo and Arthur Ray; his third son Walter Edwin and his wife Dorothy; and his fourth, fifth, and sixth sons, Ruben Daniel, Norman Earland, and Cecil Eugene, were already in North Dakota.

My father's only sister and his two living brothers attended the reunion. Lydia Reinke Middlestead lived on a farm in North Dakota. Joseph Reinke with his wife Helen came from Indiana. Emanuel "Slim" Reinke and his son Charles traveled from California.

No parent wants to outlive a child. Christian Reinke was grateful that all of his ten children were alive and healthy.

We were lucky. Three of his sons had survived World War II, although not without close calls. John, a sergeant in the Army air force, walked away from a plane crash. Emil, ever the Army private, wanting no promotion, was one of the soldiers rescued by General Patton at the "Battle of the Bulge," the German counterattack in Ardennes. Walter, in the Navy, was training to drive a LCM Landing Craft during the planned invasion of Japan.

According to Walter's expectation, the invasion of Japan was to occur in November, 1945. On August 6, 1945, the United States dropped an atomic bomb on Hiroshima. Three days later, on August 9, we exploded another in Nagasaki. On September 2, 1945, Japan surrendered unconditionally. World War II was over!

I have been in many conversations over the years with people arguing over whether Truman did the right thing when authorizing the use of atomic bombs. I always admit that I am not in a position to address the question from a moral perspective. Selfishly, I am relieved that he did. My brother Walter is alive. If it had been necessary for the United States to invade Japan, in all likelihood my brother Walter would be dead.

My father's fourth son, my brother Ruben, survived the Korean conflict. Norman and I were both in the Army. Although trained for participation, neither of us saw combat.

I've always been happy that Carol knew my dad, and that my dad knew her. When he was staying with my sister Edna in Fargo, I visited him almost daily, and often Carol came with me. She and he talked easily. He liked her. I could tell although all he ever said of her is, "She's a good girl." She observed of him, "He's such a sweet man."

Carol is the only girl I ever brought to meet my father.

My father was a man of limited schooling but unlimited wisdom. I recall one time speaking negatively of another student, someone with whom I was in competition. My dad stopped me. "Son," he cautioned, "you can't get to the top of the tree by pulling other people down." Were I a modern day politician, I would likely not be "successful." Respect for my father would not allow negative campaigning. Another time, I recall speaking "learnedly," saying something he found illogical. "Son," he said to me, "all that book learning isn't going to do you any good unless you use your common sense." No sentence since has helped me more to understand the law.

five

Near the end of my third year, when we knew that she would soon be graduated and I would be headed for law school, Carol and I talked seriously about the possibility of marriage. She was ready. I was not sure. I knew I loved Carol more than I could ever love anyone else. She was the woman I wanted with me in my old age. I could envision myself sitting beside her, holding her hand, or maybe just watching while she knitted sweaters for our grandchildren. But I was a student without financial means. I still had three years of law school to go. Ours was a simple question. Would we be together forever or go our separate ways?

Almost immediately after she graduated from North Dakota State University, on June 6, 1955, Carol traveled to California. Her discipline was dietetics, and qualification for membership in the American Dietetics Association, today, becoming a registered dietitian, requires the completion of a one year internship. Carol had applied to and been accepted as an intern by the Veterans Hospital in Los Angeles.

Before Carol left North Dakota State, her father sold his department store in Edgeley and purchased a men's clothing store in East Grand Forks, Minnesota

All three of us Reinke brothers left North Dakota State at the same time.

Ruben attended college only two years, two beneficial years. He left with an understanding of college education that would serve him well for the rest of his life. He was never to be intimidated by anyone just because the person had a college degree. He knew what a college education is, and what it isn't. Ruben did well in business. He became the most financially prosperous member of our family.

While in college Ruben met and fell in love with Marlys Yvonne Wentz. Marlys was a member of the Kappa Delta sorority. She graduated from North Dakota State with the same class that claimed Carol Roehrich. Ruben and Marlys were married shortly after her graduation. They had three children, first their son Michael Carl and later twins, a boy and girl they named Timothy Daniel and Tammy Michele. Ruben had a unique and humorous perspective on the value of children. He said to me, "I wouldn't take a million dollars for the ones I've got, and I wouldn't give a nickel for another one."

Norman decided to move to New Jersey, where our sister Edna was living. Edna left North Dakota and moved east during my third year at North Dakota State. She chose New Jersey because our oldest brother John was living there. While in New Jersey, Norman met and married Helen Marie Westog. They have five children, Melissa Margaret, Rebecca Marie, Melanie Meredith, Kathleen Amelia, and Timothy Cecil. My wife said of them, "They have the best marriage I have ever seen."

Norman became a distribution manager for one of the largest department store chains in America. After he retired, Norman and Helen built a home on the Shenandoah River in West Virginia. I love visiting them there. There is something enormously soothing about sitting on the banks of the Shenandoah, eyes resting, feeling on your face the cool, soft winds that transverse the river as if being blown by angels from heaven.

I finished my third year of college and was qualified to attend law school. While Carol was traveling to Los Angeles, I was on my way to attend ROTC camp at Fort Carson, Colorado. After completion of ROTC camp I spent the rest of the summer working for the Great Northern Railroad Company. Then it was off to law school.

Getting into law school was, for me, a very informal process. The day before classes were to start, I walked into the office of O. H. Thormodsgard, dean of the law school, and told him that I wanted to attend. I had with me a copy of my transcript from North Dakota State, showing that I had completed all of the courses prescribed for pre-law, and earned a grade point average higher than required for admission. Dean Thormodsgard looked over my transcript, asked me a few questions, and talked to me about the honorable profession of law. In one sentence he told me all about "our" law school that I would ever to need to know. "We may not produce the smartest bar," he said, "but we do produce the most honest." With that, he shook my hand and sent me upstairs to the law library where I was to take the Law School Admissions Test. The next morning, at eight o'clock, I attended my first class.

Our law school, at North Dakota University, was not very large. My first year class consisted of fewer than forty students. All subjects were mandated; there were no electives. All students of the same year sat together, in one room, for every course. Classes were conducted every weekday, Monday through Friday, from eight in the morning until noon.

Following our first day of classes, a bunch of my classmates went to the student union for lunch. Fortunately for me, I went with them. I say fortunate because it was then, while eating lunch, that I met John M. "Mike" Nilles. I had not yet found a permanent place to live. Everything I had looked at was either too expensive or too drab. Mike, I learned, was looking for a roommate. We talked, and I was accepted. Mike had found an excellent place, a basement room in a house across the street from the law school. The room was large and bright, fitted with two beds and two desks. And the price was right. Indeed, divided by two, the rent was a real bargain.

Mike Nilles was, and is, one of the best persons on earth, unashamedly religious, incorruptibly honest. A particular influence on me, as time would tell, was his self- discipline. After classes each day, Mike would take one hour for lunch. At one o'clock each afternoon, he sat at his desk and began to study. He would study until five o'clock, then break one hour for dinner. At six he would return to his desk, but not straight to study. Rather, he would light up his pipe and smoke it for about twenty minutes. Then he would put his pipe away, open his books, and study until nine. At nine o'clock each weekday he would turn off the lights on his side of the room, silently say his prayers, and go to sleep. I had no history of self-discipline, but sharing a room with Mike, I adopted his. On weekdays, with one exception, I followed his schedule. The exception was that between one and two each afternoon, I attended classes of the ROTC. Mike, having slightly more time, prepared outlines for each of our courses, which he shared with me.

The examination process in law school is different from that of any other discipline. There are no periodic tests, no mid-terms, just one comprehensive examination on each subject at the end of each semester. Because so much rides on one examination, to assist students in understanding what the tests would be like, it was the policy of our school to give practice examinations halfway through the first semester. I saw one unfortunate misreading of the results obtained on these "practice" tests. One member of our class, a young man from Texas, was elated when he saw his grades. Comparing, which no one should do, he found that his grades were higher than those of everyone else. He became convinced that he was going to be number one in our class. Following the "real" examinations at the end of the semester, he found himself somewhere near the middle. He stayed in school one more semester, after which he dropped out. As far as I know, he never became a lawyer. Better he should have heeded the old saying that prevails in all law schools: The "A" students become teachers, the "B" students become judges, and the "C" students make the money. The number one student in this class was Gerald W. VandeWalle, now Chief Justice of the North Dakota Supreme Court.

During this first year of law school, I very much missed seeing Carol.

I concentrated on my studies, trying to learn all I could about the law.

Late in this first year, an informative discussion took place in the university cafeteria that I like to relate, particularly to students with an interest in politics.

Several of my fellow students and I were sitting at a table with Usher Burdick. He was at this time still a member of Congress. As most of us knew, the man was first elected to Congress in 1935. One of my classmates asked him, "Mr. Burdick, how can anyone stay a member of Congress for twenty years?" The Congressman first replied jestingly, "Son, if you ever get a job as good as mine, you've got to be a damn fool to ever lose it." Then, respecting the question, Mr. Burdick turned serious. "I've seen a lot of politicians run out of Washington. They all lose their jobs for the one reason. They take a position that's wrong, and they try to defend it. If they would just say I made a mistake, the issue would be over. But they won't. They keep trying to defend the indefensible, digging a hole deeper and deeper until they can't get out."

Years later, while the Vietnam War was escalating, I couldn't help thinking Lyndon Johnson should have heard, from somebody, what Usher Burdick said to us.

In June, 1956, I completed my first year in law school. I was granted a bachelor degree by the University of North Dakota. At the same time, I was commissioned as a second lieutenant in the United States Army Reserve.

My brother Ruben and sister-in-law Marlys attended my graduation.

Ruben, a veteran of the Korean conflict, pinned gold bars on my Army uniform.

A photograph of the three of us, with me in the cap and gown worn during the graduation ceremony, was published in the Grand Forks Herald.

It was for me a time of pride and promise. The only thing missing was Carol.

Carol's internship was almost completed. She would be coming home!

six

We were married on September 22, 1956, in the chapel at the University of North Dakota. The ceremony was performed by Father Joseph Hylden, a long time friend of the Roehrich family. My brother Norman served as best man. Mary Helen Petersen, a sorority sister of Carol's, was the maid of honor. Both families seemed pleased with the marriage, although candidly, I think Carol's father had reservations. And perhaps he should have. Any reservations Mr. Roehrich had would have been understandable. Looking at our wedding pictures, I see a skinny kid, weighing less than one hundred thirty-five pounds, standing next to a mature, beautiful woman. Having since become the father of two girls, I know full well that there is no such thing as a man good enough to marry your daughter. I surely wouldn't have trusted one of my daughters to that kid.

A few weeks earlier, doubtless having heard something about our planning to get married, Ronnie came up to Carol and asked, "Are you really going to marry Cecil?" Telling me about this later, Carol wasn't sure exactly how she replied. Anyway, Ronnie continued. "Well, don't get me wrong, I like Cecil. If you want to marry him, that's okay. But I was thinking, if you're not going to marry Cecil, then maybe you could marry some famous baseball player." Here Carol remembered her response. "Ronnie," she said, "I don't know any famous baseball players." "Well," the fourteen-year-old concluded, semi-pleading his case, "I know a lot of girls who would do that for their brother."

There is one big advantage of long courtships. Carol and I had dated, and corresponded, for four years. We knew a lot about each other. I knew that Carol was a very strong minded person, with unshakable religious beliefs. I knew that what she most wanted was to be a mother, specifically, that she wanted seven children. I also knew that she was a very private person, that she would not like and did not want a public life.

Our courtship was of a different time, at a time when young people in love waited until marriage. As Erma Brombeck says, "We didn't get the undressed rehearsal."

Carol and I took a trip to Winnipeg, Manitoba. We had a great time. We walked the Historic Winnipeg area in the Exchange District. We saw the Forks at the confluence of the Red and Assiniboine rivers. We drove past the Royal Canadian Mint. The sights were memorable. But for me, the most memorable moment of the trip occurred as we entered Canada from the United States. At the border, a Canadian official stopped us and asked who we were. I said, "My name is Cecil Reinke. This is my wife." It was the first time I ever said, "This is my wife."

When we returned from Canada, I started my second year of law school. Carol went to work as the therapeutic dietician for St. Michael's hospital. We lived in a small apartment about a half mile from the university and slightly closer to Carol's job.

St. Michael's hospital is no more. Some years after Carol was the therapeutic dietician there, this Catholic hospital combined with a Lutheran hospital, the Deaconess. The combined hospital was called the United Hospital. It is now named the Altru Hospital and Clinic. On Columbia Road, near where St. Michael's hospital was located, there stands the University of North Dakota School of Medicine and Health Sciences.

I found a part-time job working for the athletic department of the University. It was the kind of job usually reserved for athletes. The foreman hired me because, in his mind, if he had gone to college, he would have studied law. We did such things as set up the gymnasium for events and sweep out the stadium after football games. It was not prestige work, but it paid well. Really, it was one of the best jobs on campus.

Shortly after we were married, Carol became pregnant. We were riding in a car with her father when she told him. "Hump," he grunted, "it's about time." To Nick Roehrich there was no point in our being married if not to give him grandchildren. I remember thinking, when he said it was about time, that if it had been any earlier I would have been in big trouble. We were married on September 22, 1956, and our daughter Kris was born on August 11, 1957, only ten and one-half months later.

During the second semester of my second year in law school, I was ordered to serve six months active duty in the Army, starting May 31, 1957. I was to report to Fort Benning, Georgia, on June 3. I was somewhat upset by these orders. It was not going on active duty, per se, that was disconcerting. Once I was commissioned, I knew I was obligated to serve. It was the timing. The law school semester was scheduled to end in late June, which meant that, given these orders, I would miss the last month of required study and not be present to take examinations. I went to see Dean Thormodsgard and explained my problem. To my relief, he said that I could study ahead and take all of my examinations early.

Carol and I drove from Grand Forks, North Dakota, to Columbus, Georgia, near Fort Benning. As we traveled through Kansas and Oklahoma, we were constantly alert, looking out for tornadoes. Ironically, since we never thought of tornado territory as including North Dakota, less than a month after we arrived in Columbus, the awesome tornado of June 20, 1957 destroyed much of Fargo.

As we drove through Arkansas, Mississippi, Alabama, and into Georgia, we saw the last of the worst indignities of American history. Rows of unpainted cottonwood shacks screamed of shameful economic discrimination against blacks. Even more despicable, and for which there could be no economic excuse, we saw water fountains with overhanging signs, "FOR WHITES ONLY." Alongside each spout hung a tin cup, obviously never washed, which proprietors considered "good enough" for blacks.

We rented an apartment in a complex close to Fort Benning and immediately began looking for a doctor. Carol was already in her sixth month. A number of gynecologists refused to take her as a patient, saying something about not having been able to observe her earlier progress. This was a poor excuse, I believed, because Carol had brought records from her doctor in Grand Forks. Fortunately, we did find a doctor, one of the best in Columbus, Georgia. His name was Roy Gibson. This gentleman was associated with the Columbus City Hospital. He had a daughter who was married to an Army officer. He understood.

Our neighbors were mostly second lieutenants and wives, some with children. The lieutenants were in various stages of completion of the Basic Infantry Officer Course, the training for which I was scheduled. I reported as ordered, beginning what was to be a rigorous four month grind, appropriate when you realize that we were training to possibly lead men into battle.

I learned one of the great truths about food while in training at Fort Benning. People like food they associate with good times; they dislike food they associate with bad experiences, consciously or unconsciously.

The first time I tried pizza was in Chicago, Illinois, during the summer following my first year of college. I was with a bunch of my fraternity brothers from all over the country, all of us attending a two week national leadership school sponsored by Sigma Alpha Epsilon. The school was a good experience. The guys I was with were great. I had fun while eating this first pizza. I liked pizza!

I came home one night from a long day. It was a day of competition between platoons in my company of lieutenants. We were running, jumping, chinning, and doing pushups, all in an effort to outdo the other groups. I overdid everything. Neighbors of ours, another lieutenant and his wife, suggested that Carol and I join them in going out for pizza. We went. When we got home, I got sick. I was not sick from eating the pizza; I was sick from over exercise. But it didn't matter. I no longer liked pizza. I couldn't, and didn't, eat pizza again for ten years.

My favorite food is fried potatoes. When I was a kid, sometimes when my dad would come home late from work, he and I would peel, slice and fry a big batch of potatoes. Then we'd sit together at the table, talk, and stuff ourselves with potatoes. Still today, sometimes I'll fry up a bunch of potatoes and sit down to eat them, all by myself, visiting with my father.

A few weeks after our arrival in Columbus, we were invited along with all of the other lieutenants undergoing basic infantry officer's training and the wives of those married to a Commanding General's reception. The purpose was to provide us an opportunity to meet the Fort Benning Commander. I say invited. Realistically, attendance was mandatory. Even so, it was a great party and we had fun.

Carol was at this time seven months pregnant, and she was drawing a crowd. My fellow officers who were married, and their wives, being of the reproductive age themselves, were interested in discussing the pregnancy experience. The single guys seemed fascinated. Watching her, I learned something about my wife. Although she could be the center of attention, she was never centered on herself. While talking with the crowd, she noticed a young black couple, a lieutenant and his wife, sitting alone, not talking with anybody. They looked lost, apparently feeling out of place. Carol excused herself, walked over to the couple, and literally dragged them back to the circle of officers with whom she was in conversation. A few officers, some with their wives, walked away. Most stayed, accepting in good will the participation of the new arrivals. I saw confidence grow on the couple's faces. Soon they were talking, and listening, and sharing stories, just another twosome in the circle.

Today, no one would think inviting a young black couple into a conversation to be an act of consideration. But in the year 1957, white people, especially in the south, did not commonly socialize with blacks, at least not on an "equal" basis. The civil rights movement was in its earliest stages. Hotels and restaurants were still restricted. Only eight years earlier, in 1949, had the Army adopted a new policy opening all jobs to qualified personnel without regard to race or color. The Civil Rights Act of 1964 was still seven years from enactment. Like it or not, and we did not, segregation was still the order of the day.

Feeling enormously proud of my wife, I couldn't help but whisper in wonderment, "That woman is going to be the mother of my child!"

seven

On the morning of August 11, 1957, I say for the benefit of those who understand such things, Carol's water broke. We knew the baby was coming. We spent the day counting contractions. Some of the pains, if not believed to be sufficiently strong, we neglected to count. As a result, we were almost too late getting to the hospital. Once we arrived, the nurse took one look at Carol and rushed her into the delivery room. I sat in the waiting room, visiting with another prospective father. I said earlier that the doctor we found was one of the best in Columbus. This is how I know that's true. The man spent very little time with Carol because the wife of the man I was visiting with was having a breach birth. Doctor Gibson was called upon to help, to lend his expertise to the successful completion of what was obviously a most difficult delivery.

Carol told me that the delivery was quick and easy. I knew it was quick because, not long after our arrival at the hospital, a nurse walked past me carrying a beautiful baby, with a perfectly round head. I could see the baby smiling. Her name was to be Keryl Kris Reinke. That was the name Carol wanted for our baby if we had a girl. We had a girl, born at 9: 01 p.m., August 11, 1957, in Columbus City Hospital, Columbus, Georgia, weight 7 pounds, 4 ounces, length 20 inches.

Carol also told me that, when they first brought our baby to her, she looked at the newborn and thought, "I don't know you; you're a little stranger." Then she put her hand under the baby and felt a wet diaper. It was to her like an electric shock. At that moment she felt an enormous love for this baby. She would fight a lion to protect it.

From her hospital bed, Carol called her parents with the good news. Her mother was elated. Her father said, "Put her on a bus and send her home."

A few days later there arrived at our apartment a letter addressed to "Lt. and Mrs. Cecil Reinke's daughter." It was from her grandmother, Carol's mother, Grace Roehrich:

Dear Granddaughter,

Tell your parents to let me know your name, and what you could use to wear now.

(Nick and I) your grandparents are glad you are a girl. Just wait until October you will get spoiled plenty.

Am so anxious to see you.

I don't feel any older, really a little younger, something exciting to look forward to.

Am sending your mother shorts and a bathing suit.

Uncle Ronnie says that "Marky" can be the next one.

We had over 2 inches of rain last night that was badly needed. Now everything will grow.

Washed clothes this morning. Today is a perfect day.

Tomorrow I may go up town and do a little shopping. Haven't done any for ages, have been busy packing your Uncle Bob's clothes.

Do you have a "bottle" or the good old fashioned perfect food?

Wrote to Mabel and Al, friends of ours, gave them a few surprises, marriages, phone calls, etc. They will think your mother must be "powerful," to call us on the telephone so soon after you came.

Your father's law books came yesterday. Packed them with the others in the basement.

Grow fast and get chubby because when you come here there are 4 people ready to play with you. You may even get a few fishing lessons.

Love from Grandmother, Grandfather and the Uncles.

The sentence, "Uncle Ronnie says that 'Marky' can be the next one," I should explain. Carol and I had decided that if we had a boy, we were going to name him Mark. As prospective parents do, we talked of our coming baby as if it were a boy. I cherish a large cup and saucer with the word "Father" on the cup, given to me by Carol on Christmas day, 1956, tagged as a gift from "Mark." Ronnie expected that Carol and I would have other children and that one of them would be a boy. He was just suggesting that we save the name. As it turned out, Mark was never to be. Still, he was with us those few months Carol was pregnant. We both loved him. I still love him.

The sentence, "Your father's law books came yesterday," also merits explanation. The American Law Book Company gave a volume of Corpus Juris Secundum, with name engraved on the front cover, to the law school student receiving the highest grade in any given subject of law. I received copies of volumes 10, 11, 30, 71, 77 and 78, covering Bills and Notes, Equity, Pleading, and Sales. The Lawyers Co-operative Publishing Company awarded books excerpted from American Jurisprudence. I was given books covering three subjects: Contracts, Sales, and Conflicts of Law.

The reference to "a few fishing lessons" is easiest to explain. Ronnie was an avid fisherman. He would share what he loved with the little girl he would love.

On October 5, 1957, I completed the Basic Infantry Officer's Course. My military service was not quite over. I had fifteen days leave, and orders to report to Fort Leonard Wood, Missouri, for six weeks duty as a platoon leader.

After the graduation ceremony, Carol and I with our eight week old baby entered our car and started home to Carol's parents in East Grand Forks. I did not take time to change out of my uniform. We were intent on getting home as soon as possible.

It was nearly dark when we drove into Arkansas and stopped for dinner. While we were seated in the restaurant, a gentleman approached our table and gave me the kindest and saddest of advice. I was still wearing my uniform, the uniform of an officer in the United States Army. He said to me, "Son, if I were you, I'd take off that uniform. It isn't safe." I knew immediately what he was talking about. He was talking about the recent and ongoing confrontation between the Federal Government and the State of Arkansas. He was saying that in Arkansas, at this time, it was dangerous to wear an Army uniform.

Under a federal court approved plan, Little Rock Central High School was scheduled to be integrated. The school was to open on September 3; nine black students were to attend. School officials at Little Rock demanded that these students be prevented from attending. Governor Orval Faubus backed the school officials. On September 2, Faubus ordered the Arkansas National Guard to Little Rock Central High School, allegedly to prevent violence and bloodshed, but actually to stop the black students from entering a white school. For nearly three weeks, the black children were turned away by the Arkansas National Guard.

On September 20, a Federal District Court Judge issued an injunction barring further attempts by Governor Faubus to impede integration. On September 23, no longer stopped by the Arkansas National Guard, the children, who became known throughout the world as the "Little Rock Nine," entered the school, bravely passing an ignorant mob of about 1000 whites screaming racial slurs. With the students inside, the mob became more heated. Threats were heard, reminiscent threats to drag the black children out of the school and lynch them. Within a matter of hours, probably because they wanted to, certainly without the courage displayed by the children, school officials yielded to the mob and ordered the black students out of the school. Supporters of the Little Rock Nine, concerned for the children's safety, announced that the black students would not return to the school without assurance from the President of the United States that they would receive protection from the mob.

On September 24, President Eisenhower ordered the Arkansas National Guard into active military service. That same day, he sent 1,000 paratroopers from the 101st Airborne Division at Fort Campbell, Kentucky, to protect the black children. Eisenhower's comment on the situation: "Mob rule cannot be allowed to override the decisions of our courts."

The Federal District Court Judge who ordered the integration of Little Rock Central High School was Ronald N. Davis of North Dakota.

I took the gentleman's advice. I changed out of my Army uniform for the drive through Arkansas. I say his was the kindest and sadist of advice. It was kind because the man was concerned about me, my wife, and our baby. This obviously good man wanted us to avoid attracting possible criminal actions by rabid segregationists. It was sad because I never want to believe that anyone, in any state of our union, would ever be in danger because he or she is wearing the uniform of an officer of the United States Army.

When we arrived at the home of Carol's parents in East Grand Forks, it was almost midnight. We probably should have stopped that night at a motel and completed our trip the next morning, but we were anxious to get home. We rang the doorbell, and within minutes there was Carol's father opening the front door. He took one look at us and ran back into the house to get Carol's mother, leaving us outside, with the screen door still locked. "Mother, Mother," he exclaimed "they're here. They're outside on the front porch. They've got the baby." "Well, let them in," his wife responded. Then he was back; the screen door was opened, and we stepped inside. Mrs. Roehrich immediately took charge of the baby. Nicholas J. said to his daughter, "Your mother is so excited."

In anticipation of our arrival, the Roehrichs had purchased a baby crib, one with wheels that could be rolled around in their house. They insisted that we allow the baby to sleep in their room, which was fine with us, because Carol was tired. Every night our little baby slept in the bedroom of her grandparents, and every morning her grandparents rolled her crib into the kitchen so they could look at her while they ate breakfast.

When my leave was up, I returned to duty as ordered.

The six weeks at Fort Leonard Wood, away from my wife and child, were slow going. I spent much of my free time in the Post Exchange, buying baby clothes.

There is one story from my limited platoon leader experience that I enjoy telling. One of the other platoon leaders in my company was Lieutenant Newman from Nebraska. Newman was a very bright guy, with enough charm for two. In the Army, when troops are on exercises, and eating meals cooked in the field, officers eat last. The reason is that, should there not be enough food, the shortage will be suffered not by the enlisted men but by the officers. We were in the field, all the enlisted men having been served, when Lieutenant Newman and I joined the line. Lieutenant Newman said to the cook, "Did you save me some pie?" "Yes sir," the cook responded, handing Newman a large slice. I looked at my fellow officer, slightly disapproving but greatly amused. "Newman," I said to him, "you don't understand why we're in the back of this line."

On November 30, 1957, I was released from active duty in the Army.

I started my car and drove straight, as fast as the legal limit, from the front gate at Fort Leonard Wood to the front door of the home of Mr. and Mrs. Nicholas J. Roehrich.

I was going to see my wife. I was going to see my baby.

eight

In January, 1958, I was back in law school taking out of order the work of the last semester. I liked law school, but now I just wanted it over with, done! I was acutely aware that my original classmates would be graduating in June and that I would still have one semester to go. I was feeling a complaint once uttered by Mike Nilles. "How come you have to be a professional student before you can become a professional man?"

I was pleased to learn, upon returning to school, that I had in my absence been selected an associate editor of the North Dakota Law Review. The other associate editors were John M. Nilles and Armond G. Erickson. The Editor in Chief was Gerald W. VandeWalle.

Carol had spent the last weeks of my active duty in the Army searching for an apartment. Everything she found was either inadequate or too expensive. One evening she received a call at her parent's house from Mrs. Leonard Driscoll. Mrs. Driscoll had heard that Carol was looking for an apartment. She told Carol that she had an apartment for rent, on the top floor of her house. She asked if Carol would like to see it. Carol said yes and made an appointment for the following day. When Carol told her parents about the call, her father expressed some concern. "Why would the Driscolls want to rent out an apartment in their house?" he wondered aloud. "They are millionaire potato farmers."

When Carol saw the apartment, she wanted it. Without Carol asking, Mrs. Driscoll explained why they were renting out space in their home. "The house is too big, and we don't like the upstairs empty." The rent was modest. For us, the apartment was perfect.

I found a job as a claims adjuster with one of our nation's largest automobile insurance companies. I would have less time for studying than before, but still as much time as absolutely necessary. The job paid enough so that Carol could stay home with our baby. She would not have to go back to work to keep me in law school.

My job with the insurance company was an educational experience.

After I was hired, the company assigned me to travel with and "learn the ropes" from one of their best adjusters, an elderly gentleman named Joe.

One of the claims Joe was assigned to settle was that of a man I will call Maxwell, who lived in Fargo. Maxwell, while driving his car, or more accurately, while parked at a red light sitting in his car, had been rear ended by an automobile insured by our company. We knew that the company had to pay for the damage. The only question was how much.

One evening around seven o'clock, dragging me along, Joe visited Maxwell in his home. Maxwell had three estimates of the cost of repairs that he showed to Joe and me. The lowest estimate was a little over two hundred dollars. Joe took out his company checkbook, wrote a check for the amount asked and gave it to Maxwell along with a release that Maxwell signed and Joe pocketed. The claim was settled.

I naively assumed we were ready to go. But not so. Joe stayed in his seat, drinking coffee that

Maxwell had served and continuing to talk. Joe said to Maxwell something like, "You're a very fair man, easy to do business with. Not everybody is. I'll bet you had some people advise you to ask for more, maybe even as much as two or three thousand dollars. Maybe some even suggested you claim to have been injured so you could get more." Maxwell said it was so. He acknowledged to Joe that he had been advised to "take the company for all it was worth," while proudly proclaiming that he was not that kind of man. He wanted to be fair. Joe finished his coffee. We all shook hands, and Joe and I left.

What happened next taught me a lesson I would never forget.

Within the insurance company, for each claim settled, the adjuster is required to write a report. Joe's report was a classic. He wrote that the claimant, Maxwell, had been advised to demand payment of three thousand dollars, alleging possible injuries. He implied that, using negotiation skills, he had convinced Maxwell to settle for the amount of the damage to his car.

What did this incident teach me? It taught me what Joe obviously already knew. Joe did no negotiation. He simply paid the amount requested in full. Saying this in his report would not have impressed the company with his value. By stating that Maxwell had been advised to claim much more, Joe intimated in his report that he had saved the company close to three thousand dollars, or at least the trouble of dealing with a possible claim of that amount. Joe knew, and I learned, that anyone who negotiates for someone else must make herself or himself look good, look like an able negotiator.

After this experience I was always cognizant, when negotiating with someone who was representing someone else, that the person I was negotiating with would need to render a report on the results of the negotiation. That person would want, and need, to look good in the eyes of his client or employer. So what should I do? I should make some demands that I could forgo, yield to the other negotiator. My having done so my opponent could report on something she had talked me out of, on something she had "won." I never tried to send a negotiation opponent away looking like a loser. When I could do so, at no cost to my client, I tried to make him feel like a winner. I always remembered that he would need to submit a report that would make him look like an able negotiator, make him appear to have been successful.

Also while working for this insurance company, I learned a lesson in expertise by which I have been guided all my professional life.

A small town attorney in Minnesota had a client who was badly injured in an automobile accident. The accident was caused by the negligence of a driver insured by our company. Negotiations, ongoing for months, proved fruitless. The company was offering to pay only very much less than the lawyer considered fair to his client. The thinking of the company, simply put, was this. The small town attorney was known to be a less than able trial lawyer. "Let him go to trial. He won't get much."

Once the case came to trial, my company realized it was in trouble. The small town "less than able trial lawyer" found expertise elsewhere. He brought in an excellent, high powered litigator from Minneapolis. Two results flowed. First, the small town lawyer with the help of acquired expertise won a tremendous verdict. Second, one small town attorney in Minnesota spent the rest of his legal career negotiating with my company and being accorded the respect due an experienced, capable trial lawyer.

While I was in my last year of law school, Ronnie was going to high school. Every day after school, before going home, he would visit our apartment and play with the baby. Sometimes he would stay for dinner and play with Kris some more.

The Roehrich family was crazy about "Carol and Cecil's baby."

Our little baby loved them all, welcomed being held and played with by all of them. She developed a special attachment to Carol's father, Nick, whom she was taught to call her "Papa." Little Kris loved her grandfather so much she couldn't look at him. She would look away and hold out her arms for him to take her. Only after she was in his arms could she smile and coo at him.

When the child was with her grandparents, her grandmother would sometimes taunt her about her great affection for her grandfather. She would say, "Momma's little girl, Daddy's little girl, Grandma's little girl, Uncle Bob's little girl, Uncle Jim's little girl, Ronnie's little girl," repeatedly, purposefully leaving out "Papa's little girl." Each time her grandmother went through this litany, Kris herself would add, "Papa's little girl."

During my last two semesters in law school, more than a few of my fellow students were married with small children. All the new parents were always talking about how many teeth their babies had, as if having teeth early was somehow a real accomplishment. Our baby could walk and talk in complete sentences at nine months, but she was late developing teeth. I had to listen to how "slow" she was having teeth.

On the thirty-first day of January, 1959, I was graduated from the University of North Dakota School of Law. I was admitted to the degree of Juris Doctor.

I received an offer of employment from the Little Rock District of the United States Army Corps of Engineers. Carol and I discussed the offer and decided that we would move to Arkansas. We packed our car, said goodbye to grandparents, wrapped our seventeen month old daughter comfortably in her mother's arms, and headed south.

nine

When we arrived in Arkansas, the infamous Orval Faubus was still Governor. The year before, the United States District Court ordered the integration of Little Rock Central High School. Overcoming being elbowed, poked, kicked, punched, and pushed, eight black students bravely finished the school year. One student was expelled after an altercation with a segregationist. In May, 1958, Ernest Green, the only senior of the Little Rock Nine, was graduated from Little Rock Central High School.

In August 1958, Governor Faubus called a special session of the state legislature and succeeded in having enacted a state law allowing him to close schools to prevent further integration. The following month, Faubus ordered all little Rock high schools closed. The public high schools stayed closed during all of the 1958-1959 school year. In June 1959, a Federal court declared the Arkansas school-closing law unconstitutional. Little Rock Central High School reopened in August, 1959. Several of the Little Rock Nine returned to the school. When demonstrators again descended on the school, the local police broke up the mob. The 1959-1960 school year was reasonably peaceful. Finally, integration had come to Little Rock Central High School.

Not all education occurs in the classroom. I learned a lot about economics while riding in a carpool. In my carpool back and forth to work were four engineers, all of whom had wives who were teachers at Little Rock Central High School. For the year Faubus closed the schools, all of the teachers had contracts. They were staying home, but they were still being paid. I heard such things as, "I don't care if they never open the schools again; I'd never let them in." Within a few months, these engineers came to understand that if the high schools stayed closed for another year their wives would not be paid. Suddenly, I was hearing things like, "Well, it wouldn't hurt to let a few in." Praises be to Martin Luther King, who best understood that the way to motivate a bigot is to hit him in the pocketbook.

While working in Little Rock, under date of March 24, 1959, I received from Dean O. H. Thormodsgard a most welcome letter. This is what he wrote:

Mr. Cecil E. Reinke
Apt. 4, 1019 Cavanaugh
Little Rock, Arkansas

Dear Mr. Reinke:

Congratulations to you! You are fourth in a class of 39 students as to scholarship and hence, you merit election to the Order of The Coif. We are very pleased that you are one who succeeded to this honor. The Annual Dinner meeting of the Order of The Coif will be held on May 1, which is Law Day. The Honorable Edward J. Devitt, Federal District Court Judge of St. Paul, Minnesota, who was a graduate in

1935, was elected Honorary Member. He will give the main address. Miller, Rahlfs, and Orban will also give a six-minute talk on some specific important law topic. If you plan to attend the Coif Dinner, be prepared to give a six-minute talk.

With honors, there comes responsibility and burdens. The only fee to become a member of the Order of The Coif is $25 which is paid only once. That pays for the certificate, the 14x Coif Key, and a copy of the Constitution and by-laws and the history of The Coif. If you unfortunately cannot attend the dinner, in fairness to you, the fee will be only $22 in that three dollars is used in payment of the Annual Dinner.

The Law Faculty extends to you its best wishes. We may see you this summer when you take the Bar Examination on July 14. Perhaps we may see you on May 1. I trust that you will be able to pay the above fee of $25 or $22 some time during the next forty days. We will mail to you, by registered mail, the Coif Key and certificate shortly after Law Day. We are ordering those certificates, etc., today.

With kind personal regards, I remain

Sincerely yours, O. H. Thormodsgard, Dean

Admission to the Order of The Coif was the apex of my law school experience. Candidly, when I was graduated, I did not think I would qualify. I had thought I was one of the top three students in the law school class I started with, but everyone in that class except me had been graduated in June of 1958. During my last semester, when I felt alone and out of place, the grades I earned were not up to par. I was pleased to learn later that in the class of 1959 I actually finished third.

I did not attend the annual dinner. I gladly paid the required membership fee.

An amusing exchange of correspondence took place while I was preparing my application to take the North Dakota bar examination. I asked Gene Kruger, a good friend of mine and long time friend of Carol and her brothers, to give me one of the required character references. Gene was the son of the "Mabel and Al" mentioned in Carol's mother's letter to "Lt. and Mrs. Reinke's daughter." He had been a third year law student at North Dakota University when I was in my first year. He was at this time a practicing attorney in Fargo. He was later to become the District Attorney for Cass County. Gene Kruger provided the required attestation to my good moral character with one "reservation," as seen in this excerpt from his letter, dated May 28, 1959:

Enclosed is Exhibit "5" which I have filled out and signed for your use in your application to the Bar Association. Since I have had no word of any direct association of you with Faubus, I am willing to attest to your good moral character. However, should your conscience bother you on this, please be good enough to give me the opportunity to retract my affidavit.

I responded to Gene's letter on June 5, writing to him, in part:

I have received the form relative to my application for admission to the North Dakota Bar Association which you were kind enough to complete and return to me. I wish to express my thanks and appreciation for your consideration in this regard. Your promptness in returning the form has left an abundance of time in which to forward my complete application to Bismarck.

Please rest assured that were I so lacking in intelligence and moral fortitude as to be a supporter of Mr. Faubus, I would not be so presumptuous as to put myself forward as one qualified to apply for examination and admittance to membership in Dean Thormodsgard's "most honest" Bar Association.

On July 14, 1959, in Bismarck, North Dakota, I took the North Dakota bar examination. I was admitted to the Supreme Court of the State of North Dakota on July 17, 1959.

Living in Arkansas, I decided to apply for admission to the Arkansas Bar Association. I took the Arkansas bar examination, passed, and was granted a license to practice before the Supreme Court of the State of Arkansas on April 4, 1960.

A unique "opportunity" was afforded me a few days later. In Little Rock, at that time, it was the practice of the local bar association to sponsor a dinner in honor of newly admitted members. I was sitting at a table, enjoying the dinner, when someone tapped me on the shoulder and asked if I would go into another room to "see Judge Smith." Judge Smith was a practicing lawyer in Little Rock, who had served a brief period as a Justice of the Arkansas Supreme Court. Judge Smith asked me if I would like a job as personal secretary to Orval Faubus. I said, "No sir, I am committed to the Corps of Engineers."

I did not want to have to return Gene Kruger's character affidavit.

ten

We very much enjoyed our life in Little Rock. Arkansas is a wonderful state.

Upon arrival in Little Rock, we rented an apartment in a quadriplex on Kavanaugh Street. We were on the ground floor. Above us lived the Elwoods, Jim and Genelle, who had a daughter Janna the same age as Kris. Jim was a salesman for the Kleenex Company. Just across a walkway from our front door lived another couple, Wayne and Carol Ann Cushing. Wayne was a student in medical school at the University of Arkansas for Medical Sciences in Little Rock.

We developed a deep and lasting friendship with Wayne and Carol Ann.

One night the four of us -- Carol Ann, Wayne, Carol and I -- were reminiscing about the colleges we attended. We regaled each other with tales of who was there, what certain faculty members were like, things we did, pranks pulled, and uproarious fun we had. Caught up in the mood, Carol Ann said something I was never to let her forget. She sighed, "I wouldn't give up my school for all the education I could have gotten somewhere else."

We were none of us so ignorant as to hear Carol Ann's comment as an affront to her college. It was praise. We took her comment for what it was, enthusiasm for a great school. Florida Southern College in Lakeland may have something it could be ashamed of but, if it does, it is not the quality of the education provided Carol Ann Cushing.

One evening I was talking with our now eighteen month old daughter about somewhere she had gone. I said to her, "Kris, you can't trespass on other people's property." Carol Ann was amazed. "Trespass? You talk to the kid with words like that?"

Some days after we moved into this apartment, I was carrying in groceries. As I came through the door, something slipped, and down went a dozen eggs, all broken, running white and yellow. Our little Kris was standing close to me, and soon Carol appeared. I exclaimed wrongfully, "That darn kid." My child, truthfully, turned to her mother and said, with her very small voice but ample vocabulary, "I did not do that. My daddy did that all by himself."

Kris had a doll she called "Ruthie." She carried it around by the hair. Most of the hair disappeared. One evening Kris said to her mother, "Ruthie doll does not have pretty hair."

Carol took Kris to a pediatrician, Dr. J. E. Jones. She said to Dr. Jones, "Look at the way this child walks." Dr. Jones said, "She walks very well." Carol insisted, "You know that's not what I mean." "Oh," the doctor responded, "you mean the pronation. We can fix that." The doctor prescribed special shoes for Kris to wear, shoes that would condition her to walk with feet evenly on the ground. Still today I sometimes look at Kris' shoes. They are always evenly worn, no more on one side than the other.

Once when Kris was sick, Dr. Jones came to our apartment. Earlier he had been upstairs caring for Janna Elwood. Ours were the last days when doctors made house calls. Dr. Jones said to our little girl, "I've just been up to see Janna; she's feeling better." Kris told the doctor, "You just go back, see Janna Elwood. Krissy no like you."

When our daughter Kris reached two years of age, Carol decided to put her in a nursery school and go back to employment. She was offered and accepted a therapeutic dietetic position with the University of Arkansas for Medical Sciences in Little Rock.

We were nervous about the idea of leaving our daughter in a nursery school, afraid that she might cry. As happened, Kris took one look at all the kids in the school and ran right in, never looking back. She was so accepting that Carol and I felt a little rejected. Only one time during nearly two years in "Mrs. Duke's Nursery School" did Kris come home with something we thought might be a complaint. Talking about what happened that day she said, "A boy knocked me down." Concerned, we inquired if she was mad at the boy. "No," she said, "he told me if I didn't stop he was going to knock me down." "What were you doing?" we asked. "I was slapping him in face with hand."

When Kris started nursery school, Mrs. Duke asked her name. During the first months of her life, Carol's parents and brothers, and we too, referred to her as "Krissy Goo." So Kris told Mrs. Duke, "My name is Krissy Goo Reinke." Later, Mrs. Duke came to know that "Goo" was not part of the child's name.

When she was two years old, Kris had her adenoids and tonsils removed. After the operation, Mrs. Duke gave her a doll. We called the doll "Adenoids Duke." It became for Kris a favorite.

We bought Kris a Chatty Kathy doll. You pull a string and it talks. Kris pulled the string. The doll said, "I love you." Kris was convinced, "She likes me!"

In one of the apartments of our quadriplex lived an attorney about my age who worked for the Arkansas Attorney General. He came home one evening and found Carol and Genelle Elwood outside visiting. He said to Genelle, "Hello Sweetheart." He said to Carol, "Hello Mrs. Reinke."

When Kris was three, we took her to a Little Rock city park where they were giving horse rides to children. They were small horses, Shetland ponies if I'm correct. They were tied to a hot walker and paced slowly in circles. As we crossed the park grounds on our way to where the horses were located, Kris was determined. "I'm gonna ride that horsey. I'm gonna ride that horsey. I'm gonna ride that horsey," she repeated with every step. When we got there, Kris looked at what was confronting her. "My, that's a big horsey," she balked. We went home. The next day we returned, and Kris rode the horse.

Carol accomplished one thing while working at the medical center of which I am most proud. In the kitchen, all the workers were black, but all the "supervisors" were white. Carol observed that most of the workers knew more than the supervisors. A vacancy occurred when one of the supervisors quit. Carol approached the Chief Dietitian, Mrs. Nell Jane McCormick, and suggested that they select one of the black women to serve as a supervisor. Mrs. McCormick agreed. Carol then talked with the woman they decided to appoint, knowing that she would be nervous about the idea, assuring her that she would do well. A significant color barrier was broken!

From her workplace at the hospital, Carol brought me the "legal case" that in my mind justifies my becoming a lawyer. One of the workers in the hospital kitchen was having trouble with the Internal Revenue Service. They said that she owed some amount of income taxes, which she had no money to pay. She offered to pay in increments, but her offer was rejected. She didn't know what to do, so she came to Carol. Carol said she would talk to her husband, and that night she did. "I hope you don't mind," she started, "but I promised your legal help to someone." She then told me the story. I asked about the woman, what she did, how much money she earned. "She only earns $100 a month, and her husband has no income. He's a mental patient in the Arkansas State Hospital." My immediate thought was, how can the lady owe any income taxes? There was at that time a $600 personal exemption. For a husband and wife, the exemption was $1,200. That's all the woman earns. The next day I went to the hospital and had the woman sign an authorization for me to look at her file and submit an amended return. The woman got a tax rebate!

One day while I was busy working, Cecil Kuehnert came to the front of my desk and said he had a job for me. Mr. Kuehnert was the Little Rock District Counsel, my boss. At first I assumed that he was talking about a legal problem, but that wasn't it. He had received a call from E. Manning Seltzer, Chief Counsel of the Corps of Engineers in Washington, D. C. There was an attorney vacancy in the Office of the General Counsel, Office of the Secretary of the Army, in the Pentagon. There was also a dispute concerning how to fill the vacancy, between the General Counsel, Powell Pierpoint, and the Deputy General Counsel, William Compton. Mr. Pierpoint wanted to hire someone from a private law firm, presumably from New York. He believed there were no good lawyers working for the Army. Mr. Compton was concerned about his career development program, a plan he initiated to recruit and train excellent lawyers in house. Mr. Compton, incidentally, was a former professor at Georgetown. He wrote the casebook on domestic relations that I used in law school. He had come to the Office of the General Counsel during World War II and stayed after the war was over. Mr. Seltzer supported Mr. Compton's position. Mr. Seltzer wanted me to apply because he thought I had an excellent chance of being selected.

I talked with Carol about this situation. She said it was up to me; if I wanted to move to Washington, she would go. It was the hardest and the most ill considered career decision I ever made. We liked Little Rock. We liked living in Little Rock. We had good friends in Little Rock. I decided to apply.

A few days later I flew to Washington, walked into the Pentagon, and submitted myself to interviews by both Powell Pierpoint and William Compton. Then I flew back to Little Rock to await their decision. Less than a week later I received a telephone call from Mr. Compton. I was offered a job as an Assistant to the General Counsel, Office of the Secretary of the Army.

There is one thing I specifically remember about our drive to Washington. We were almost there, somewhere in Virginia, when I made some kind of driving error. A patrolman pulled us over. He asked to see my driver's license. I showed it to him. He asked to see our automobile registration. I could not produce one. He said to me, "How do I know this is your car?" Suddenly, from the back seat, the small voice of our three-year-old was heard to say, "Dis is too our car."

The patrolman waved us on our way.

eleven

I liked working in Washington. There is something exhilarating about working on an issue during the day and reading about it in the newspaper at night.

John Fitzgerald Kennedy was President of the United States. The city was considered to be populated by "the best and the brightest."

I learned something about columnists. What they write is often inaccurate.

I learned a little about Washington life. I learned, for example, that when somebody says, "Ev said," that person does not know Senator Dirksen. When someone says, "Senator Dirksen said," he or she may very well know the Senator. I learned that in Washington, people don't bribe with money; they bribe with association. I marveled that people in the Pentagon would become ecstatic because some Senator, Congressman, White House official, or prominent lobbyist called them by their first names. The message to these government workers is, if you want me to recognize you, "be good."

I learned indirectly that the Deputy General Counsel, William Compton, judged dog shows. Another Assistant to the General Counsel, who shall remain nameless, was telling me about the performance appraisal given him by Mr. Compton. He was not rated as highly as he would like to have been, so he went to see his appraiser to ask why. "What's wrong me as a lawyer?" Mr. Compton said to him something like, "Look, you're happy with yourself, leave it be. I judge dog shows and one thing I've learned. The people that enter their dog think that it is perfect. If I told them what was wrong with their dog, they would never see it quite the same again." Frustrated, the guy said to me, "I went to see Mr. Compton. He compared me to a dog."

One of the most memorable days of my Pentagon experience is February 20, 1962, the day John Glenn in the Mercury spacecraft Friendship 7 three times orbited the earth. Work within the building seemingly came to a standstill. Everybody including me was glued to a television set, tensely rooting for the success of the mission, and pleading for Glenn's safe return to solid ground.

While living in Washington, because the opportunity was there, I took a couple of graduate courses at the Georgetown University School of Law. This kept me away from home two evenings for several weeks. Carol was okay with this, but interestingly, she began to notice that my evening absences appeared to upset our daughter Kris. One evening, while I was attending class, the mother confronted her little daughter.

"What is it, Honey? What's making you unhappy? Is it just that you miss your father?"

"Well," our troubled little four-year-old girl complained, "I don't think it's fair that some people who are lawyers get to go to more school, while other people haven't even been to Kindergarten yet."

Among the neighbors we had while I worked in the Pentagon were Henry and Ellen Morgenstern. Henry was a lawyer who worked for the State Department. Henry's family, all except his grandmother, escaped from Hitler-occupied Belgium. Henry's grandmother delayed leaving to take in her laundry. They never heard from her again.

Carol and I spent a lot of time with and very much liked Henry and Ellie Morgenstern. One day our little daughter overheard a racial slur about Jews. She mentioned what she had heard to her mother. "Don't pay any attention to that," Carol told Kris. "People who say things like that are just plain stupid." She tried to explain in words a bright four-year-old could understand, "Being a Jew just means you go to church. They don't go to the same church we do, but they go to a good church." Carol was thankful she had proof. "Henry and Ellen Morgenstern are Jews."

We did not like living in Washington. Carol and I were not of the "Martini set."

From what I saw, most of the people who lived and worked in Washington were there "temporarily." They considered some place else to be "home." I remember talking with a more senior employee in the Pentagon, a man with a wife and two teenage boys, about what he was going to do after retirement. "I'm going to move back home to Texas." Do you go home often, I asked. "No, actually, I haven't been home since I came to Washington." How long have you been in Washington? "Twenty years." I remember thinking, and questioning. The man's been here twenty years and Texas is his home? He has two sons that have never been to Texas. Where is their home?

One thing we did like about Washington, D. C., was its location. It was close to New Jersey, where my sister Edna and brothers John and Norman lived, and not too far from Rhode Island, where my sister Ruth lived. Visiting back and forth with them was made easier.

I visited with my brother John while he was working. John operated a small gasoline station just outside of Philadelphia. It was not the normal gas station that we are used to seeing. It had no garage, in fact, no substantial building at all, just a little hut he could sit in to keep warm. It had no islands of gasoline pumps, only two pumps. I asked him, "Johnny, how can you make a living with this?" "Well, Cecil," he explained, "it's like this. When someone drives in here to buy gas, I talk with him, or her. I get to know his name. If you can call a customer by name, he'll drive ten miles out of his way to buy gas from you."

My brother John made enough money at that small gas station to put three kids through the University of Oklahoma.

In small families, with only two, three, or four siblings, get-togethers are called visits. In large families like that of my parents, Christian and Fredericka Reinke, get-togethers are called reunions. Every few years, one of my brothers or sisters would invite all of us to a "reunion." Reunions were held in Clinton, Oklahoma, where my sister Lydia lived; in Helena, Montana, where my brother Walter and his wife Dorothy moved when they left North Dakota; in Idaho Falls, Idaho, where my brother Ruben lived; and in Charles Town, West Virginia, where my brother Norman built his retirement home on the Shenandoah River. The last reunion that Carol attended, called after we learned she had terminal cancer, was held at my sister Ruth's home in Warwick, Rhode Island.

After more than a year in Washington, Carol and I decided to leave.

I found an available job in Orlando, Florida, the position of Counsel for the Orlando Branch Office of the U. S. Army Missile Command. It was a city we thought we would like. It was a job I thought I would like. I applied and was selected.

I started work at my new job on August 1, 1962.

Shortly after we arrived in Orlando, we bought a home in Sky Lake, a subdivision about five miles south of city center.

Much to her delight, we put Kris in kindergarten.

twelve

One day, shortly after we moved to Orlando, Carol and I were sitting at our kitchen table talking when she asked me, "Cecil, what would you think about our adopting a baby girl?" I did not respond with something stupid like "I don't know; what would you think?" I knew what she thought. I had known from the earliest days of our courtship that she wanted a large family. Seven children had been her target. We'd been married for six years, and still had only one child. Both Carol and I had been to doctors, intent on finding what was wrong. "Nothing is wrong," the doctors said. "We can find nothing wrong with either of you." Yet nothing happened. Years passed and we had no more children. So I knew what my wife wanted. She wanted another child. I said to her, quietly and simply, "Honey, I think that would be a good idea." As turned out, it was not only a good idea, it was a great idea. It was the best idea that Carol or I, or both of us together, ever had.

Almost immediately after Carol and I first decided that we would try to adopt a baby, Carol began discussing the possible adoption with Kris, who was then five years old. Our girl liked the idea of having a baby sister, but she had one concern. She looked at Carol, with big brown eyes dominating a little face that was both questioning and serious, and asked, "How are you going to get that baby away from its mother?"

Carol told her that the baby did not have a mother.

Kris wanted to know, "Why doesn't the baby have a mother?"

Carol tried to explain. "We really don't know why, honey," she told Kris. Things happen. Sometimes people die. And sometimes, someone has a baby that she just can't keep, that she can't take care of. All we really know is that this baby doesn't have a mother. She needs a mother. I need another baby. Your dad needs another child. The baby that we want to get needs both a mother and a father. And she will want you to be her sister.

Carol did essentially all of the work necessary to adopt a baby. It was she that contacted Catholic Charities, the agency from which we adopted our girl. It was she that picked up the application forms, which we filled out together. It was she that scheduled our interviews with the social workers, so they could look us over.

I remember in particular part of one of our interviews. The social worker seemed hesitant. She said to Carol, "I don't know, you seem awfully wrapped up in the one child you have." To which Carol responded, "Are you telling me that if I didn't like the child I've got, that I would be a better candidate?" The social worker, I was pleased to see, wisely realized that she had expressed a senseless concern.

We were approved. And then we had to wait. Wait we did, for almost six months. Finally, the call came. "We have a girl for you," the social worker said. Carol was ecstatic. "Only one thing wrong with her," the social worker continued, "she has red hair."

Carol determined, "That's nothing wrong."

"Of course," the social worker went on, "the daughter you have is kind of red-headed, isn't she."

Our Kris, at that time, was a pure blonde.

"We want her," Carol said. "When can we get her?"

"Not right away," the social worker answered. "We're bringing her in from Tampa. It will take another week or so."

A meeting was set for Monday, August 5, 1963.

The next week, the week before we were scheduled to get our baby, I had to travel to Huntsville, Alabama, on business. Carol and Kris went with me. Carol and I were as excited and nervous as two young people could be. We spent all our spare time shopping for baby clothes.

The day finally came, the day we were going to get our baby!

The two of us, Carol and I, were sitting in the lounge, anxious for them to bring us our baby. We were nervous, feeling fidgety but sitting still, waiting. The door opened and in walked a woman carrying a baby. She wasn't a newborn. She was seven months old. She was dressed in a little pink dress and bottom that Carol saved, saved for the day when we would give it to her. The woman took only a few steps and placed the baby on Carol's lap. Carol later said she almost couldn't believe it. This little bundle was going to be ours. Looking at the baby, I thought she had a deformed lip. I remember thinking, they didn't tell us about that, but so what, that's no reason to reject a baby. Carol, of course, saw no deformed lip. What she saw was what we actually got, the most beautiful baby that ever there was. What I saw as a deformed lip, Carol later explained, was a baby teething and pulling in her lips.

We drove the baby right home, and there was Kris, waiting on our driveway.

I remember Carol asking me, "Can they ever take this baby away from us?" "No," I assured her. "This is our child. We're going to be good parents. No power can ever take her from us."

At the time, as a lawyer, I was telling my wife the truth. That was and still should be the law.

Only later did some judges, who fail to understand, issue rulings that have undermined the adoption process.

One thing I've always said about children, jestingly, with purposeful reversal of a basic truth, is that "they can't stand security." Let me explain. A child that is neglected and abused will fall all over itself trying to earn the approval of its parents. A child that knows its parents love it more than their own lives is inevitably sassy and demanding. Carol and I had sassy and demanding children. We have sassy and demanding grandchildren. By sassy and demanding, I mean assertive. Sassy and demanding is not the same as spoiled. Spoiled children have no discipline. Sassy and demanding children have considerable personal discipline. They have strength and self-confidence. Our grandchildren are not spoiled. Our children were not spoiled. As my daughter Kris says, to this day, "We were not spoiled; we were catered to." I wanted my children raised with self-discipline, strength, and self-confidence. I want my grandchildren raised with self-discipline, strength, and self-confidence. I value self-esteem. I like sassy and demanding.

Three days, that's all it took. After three days our baby knew she was loved. She became sassy and demanding. She wanted to be held all the time, and we held her all she wanted. She was our girl!

Possibly, although I do not know, she had been bounced around for the first seven months of her life. When our neighbors first came to see her, she screamed bloody murder. The first time the social worker came, she screamed. I remember thinking that she thought the people were coming to take her away. I told the social worker, right out, "I believe the baby is afraid you're going to take her away." I still think I was right. After a few weeks anyone who wanted to could come into our home, including the social worker, and the baby would not scream. She came to know that we were not going to let anybody take her away.

She had red hair, but not your ordinary washed out red. It was the prettiest hair color I have ever seen, a dark, rich shade of red that I had never seen before and have seen only twice since. We named her Alison Dale Reinke. Most of the time, we called her Al, or Ally. Later on, when she was being a pest her sister Kris called her "Finko," much to her irritation. I loved referring to her as "Little Red Alison."

Our friend Carol Ann Cushing said of Alison, "She's the prettiest baby I have ever seen."

It took Kris some time, I believe, to really understand that in getting Alison we had done nothing wrong. An incident that occurred in a grocery store is indicative. Carol was shopping with our two kids along, Alison belted safely in a grocery cart, when an elderly gentleman came near the cart said something like, "My, what a beautiful baby, I think I'll take her home." Kris jumped between the man and the cart and exclaimed, "That's our baby, and you better leave her alone or I'm calling my mom." "Honey," the man said to Kris, doubtless surprised by her overreaction, "I wouldn't take your baby."

At the time we got Alison, we were living in the Sky Lake subdivision. There lived in our neighborhood a woman who had two little red-headed girls, ages about three and five. These little girls regularly walked the two blocks from their home to our house and asked to see our new baby. They were obviously fascinated by the fact that Alison, like them, had red hair. One day their mother came with them. "They think there must have been some kind of mistake," the woman explained to Carol. "They think the baby belongs in our house. I told them that we could get another baby, but that we would have to get the daddy first."

The social worker that said of Alison, "Only one thing wrong with her, she has red hair," forever affected my sense of humor. All her life Alison has heard me say, in loving remembrance,

"There's only one thing wrong with you, kid. You've got red hair."

Alison was born on December 17, 1962, in Tampa, Florida. Carol and I got her on August 5, 1963. Each seventeenth of December we celebrate her birthday. Every year on the fifth of August we celebrate what Carol designated "I Got You Day."

Sometimes in life, if you're extremely fortunate, you can claim more happiness than nature intended. Carol and I were extremely fortunate. We got Alison.

thirteen

Kris learned to read in Kindergarten. How she learned to read I never understood. You expect kids to come to you from time to time with questions. "What's this word?" "What's that word?" Kris never did. Reading came to her naturally. Overnight, it seemed, she was reading copiously. She was almost never without a book in her hands.

She liked school at first but soon found the experience frustrating.

One time Kris went to the school library and wanted to take out a book. The librarian wouldn't give it to her. "That's too hard a book for a second grader. Let me find you something else." Kris knew she could read the book but she didn't argue with the woman. She just left. When she got home she told her mother. Carol went to the school and got the book.

When our kids were in grade school, the educators were doing what I suppose grade schools are still doing. They were separating children into rooms based on their perception of how bright they were. Of course, the schools didn't say, this room is for the smart kids, that room is for the others. They resorted to euphemisms, but the kids knew. The fact that children understand what is being done with them is in and of itself sufficient reason, in my judgment, to condemn the practice.

In Kris' second grade class the children were divided into Redbirds and Bluebirds.

Kris came home with her report card, her grade in every subject a Satisfactory. Her mother and I, as young parents will, were falling all over ourselves praising her good school work. "Satisfactory in every subject; that's just great!" we acclaimed. Our second grader scoffed, "Isn't this silly. Of course, I'm a satisfactory Redbird. If I wasn't a satisfactory Redbird I'd be a Bluebird."

One evening while Carol's parents were visiting the telephone rang. Carol's mother answered. The woman identified herself as "Keryl's teacher." "Are you Keryl's mother?" the teacher asked. Grace Roehich, hearing the woman saying "Keryl," pronounced the same as the name Carol, answered yes. She was surprised to hear from "Carol's teacher," but accepting. She was cognizant that her daughter Carol, my wife and Keryl Kris' mother, was at this time attending an adult sewing course.

"Keryl's a real smart girl, isn't she," the teacher said.

Mrs. Roehrich, somewhat perplexed, answers, "Yes, of course she is."

"But she plays around a lot."

"What?" Carol's mother exclaims.

"Sometimes when I call on her, I find that she is not paying attention."

"Well," Carol's mother told the woman, totally frustrated but finally realizing that she was talking with her granddaughter's teacher, not her daughter's, "if you're calling her Keryl no wonder she's not paying attention, we call her Kris."

When Kris was in the fourth grade, the teacher handed out an assignment. It was a list of words. The children were told to go home and look up the meaning of any of the words they did not know. The next day Kris handed in a blank sheet of paper.

The teacher said to her, "You didn't do the assignment."

"Yes I did," Kris responded.

The teacher said, "I'm not sure I know all these words."

Kris commented, "You may not, but I do."

This teacher later said of Kris, "If the President of the United States came into our classroom, he'd sure get his comeuppance." I was not disappointed to hear this. I wanted our children sufficiently confident to be comfortable talking with teachers, principals, neighbors, working people, and Presidents, with equal directness and courtesy.

Another teacher told Carol about something Kris did. A child in the class was hospitalized. The teacher suggested that they each make a get well card to send to him. All the children came forward to take some construction paper. Everyone except Kris selected paper of a bright color—red, green, or yellow. Kris selected black. The teacher thought, that Kris! Then she saw. Kris took a scissors and cut the perfect image of a bat. On the card in white letters she wrote, "You're driving me bats. Fly out of that hospital."

A teacher became upset when she heard Kris say the word "Goobers," thinking it distasteful. She learned that Kris was talking about peanuts.

Our second year in Orlando, Carol decided that our children needed swimming lessons. We did not have a swimming pool, but many people did. Carol thought the kids would be safer if they could swim. Carol found professional lessons given at one of the larger hotels in downtown Orlando by a former Olympic swimmer from, I believe, Bulgaria. Kris was okay with taking the lessons, and she soon learned to swim. She was never a strong swimmer, but she is a beautiful swimmer, with proper kick and arm movements. Alison hated the lessons. She called them "lady lessons" because the instructor was a woman. When Carol took the kids to the hotel, Alison would go reluctantly to the pool holding her mother's hand pleading, "No lady lessons. No lady lessons." The instructor understood children. I watched the way she handled one child she judged to be frightened of the water, very gently lowering her into the water and snuggly bringing her out. I saw how she handled Alison. She would throw our child into the water, telling her she would have to make her way back to the edge of the pool. When the instructor lifted her out of the pool, Alison would be screaming in protest. "She's not scared," the woman told Carol, "she's just mad." The lady was obviously right. At age two Alison could swim like a little fish. I still take great pleasure in watching old home movies showing our Little Red Alison swimming to me, her father.

When she first learned to swim, Alison was not yet able to breathe while swimming. I would get into the pool with her. She would swim to me, and I would lift her out of the water. She always swam with her eyes open. Once some other child asked, "Why do you swim with your eyes open?" Alison answered, "You have to have eyes open to see your daddy."

Carol's parents loved little Alison. They thought her a little doll.

Her "Papa," Grandfather Nick, taught her to spell her name. He did it by singing with her the letters "A-l-i-s-o-n" to a made up melody, with the "o" as a high note.

Alison was a little dickens.

We improved our house by adding a new bathroom window. The new window was only two days old when, on an evening that I was away attending a meeting of the Army reserve, two year old Alison went into the bathroom and locked the door. Her mother called for her to open the door. No response. Carol tried to open the door with the emergency access key that works from the outside. The key wouldn't work! Alarmed, Carol ran to the house next door to get help. She asked our neighbor, Ding Bell, to please break the window. Mr. Bell broke the window. One glance inside and our neighbor knew immediately why the access key did not work What he saw was our Little Red Alison standing with her finger against the inside button on the doorknob.

The little dickens was also a roamer.

The moment we lost sight of her she was out of our yard.

Near the entrance to the Sky Lake subdivision is a small creek with a bridge over it, very little water but dangerous nonetheless. I can't count how many times I went running to the bridge. To my repeated great relief, it was never for Alison a destination.

While we lived in Sky Lake, life in the suburbs was a different experience than is living in a subdivision today. In almost every house there lived a one-income family. Fathers went to work and mothers stayed home. Our neighborhood was replete with children. All the mothers looked out for their own children, and for the children of others. When Alison slipped away from our watch, what we worried about was the creek. We never worried about human predators. I have a Webster's New Collegiate Dictionary from 1960 that doesn't list the word "pedophile." Today, we live in a nation of two-income families. Families still live in the suburbs, but there are few mothers at home all day. Most young mothers have to be employed outside the home in order to satisfy family financial obligations. There are few children playing in yards. Parents take their children to nursery schools else they would have not many others with which to play.

One night our little red-head got out of her bed around two o'clock in the morning, went out our front door, and rang the doorbell of the Bell's house next door. Ding and Louise Bell brought her home. The next day I put dead bolts on the upper corners of the outside doors.

Alison obviously relished her proclivity as a roamer. When she was three or four years old, she had a ukulele. She liked to make up songs, her own tunes and lyrics. One of the songs she regularly sang, to a tune I can still hear, had these words:

My mother came home, home, home.

She didn't even find her girl, girl, girl.

She went to the neighborhoods, hoods, hoods.

She found her girl, girl, girl.

fourteen

We were living in Florida during the Cuban Missile Crisis of October, 1962, "the week that shook the world." The reality of the danger was especially pronounced to us and our neighbors. Outside, day and night, we could hear the roar of military planes, seemingly hundreds of them. The roar ended only after Khrushchev agreed to stop work on missile sites in Cuba and ship all weapons back to the Soviet Union.

We were living in Florida on that awful day, November 22, 1963, when President John F. Kennedy was shot in Dallas, Texas. Carol heard the news on the radio and immediately turned on the television. She called me at my office, having confirmed what she heard. I came right home. We wanted not to believe the unbelievable. We cried with Walter Cronkite as he announced that the President of the United States of America was dead:

From Dallas, Texas, the flash -- apparently official.

President Kennedy died at 1:00 p.m. Central standard time, 2:00 p.m. Eastern standard time, some 38 minutes ago.

President Kennedy should have lived to see the fulfillment of his boldest initiative. On May 25, 1961, he told a joint session of Congress: "I believe this nation should commit itself to achieving the goal, before this decade is out, of landing a man on the moon and returning him safely to earth." This nation was inspired by Kennedy's vision. The otherwise unimaginable was achieved. Before the decade was out, on July 20, 1969, two American astronauts, Neil A. Armstrong and Edwin E. Aldrin, Jr., landed on the moon, walked on the moon, and returned safely to earth.

While we were living in Florida, Carol's brother Ronnie visited us often, first as a college student at the University of Arkansas, later as a candidate in training at Pensacola, and finally as on officer of the United States Navy. He spent his last Christmas enjoying our children. Kris and Alison got to know him very well.

Shortly after we adopted Alison, he came to see her. Alison jumped into his arms. He said to Carol, "I would have liked her anyway, but she really likes me."

Ronnie took our daughter Kris out on a "date." She was seven or eight years old. He invited her for dinner and a movie. He took her in his small white convertible, with the top down. They got home around nine o'clock. Kris was asleep in the car. Ronnie carried her into the house. He said to Carol and me, "I'm hard on a date."

Ronnie had become totally ambidextrous. He was always fairly ambidextrous. When playing baseball, he was a right handed batter, but a left handed thrower. The reason he threw with his left is that, when he was a grade school student, he found in his home a baseball mitt that fitted onto his right hand. When he was in the eighth grade, he broke his right arm. By the time it healed, he was equally adept at using either hand. He could write with both hands, do anything else with either hand. While visiting us during his senior year at the University of Arkansas, he was painting the ceiling in our Sky Lake house. Carol said to him, "Ronnie, when you get tired take a break." His response, "I'm okay. When I get tired, I just paint with the other hand."

After about four years living in Sky Lake, we purchased a larger house in an Orlando subdivision known as Lake Conway Estates. Ronnie came down from Pensacola to help us move. I had hired a carpenter to make a bookcase of a specific size, which was delivered while we were moving into our new home. The carpenter was an artist. I was and still am happy with his work. Carol, Ronnie, and I were outside saying goodnight to the man when he said, "This is one of my last jobs. I'm going to retire and pursue my hobby." Carol asked the question that should never have been asked. "What is your hobby?" His hobby was coin collecting. He had in his van a great number of coins that he insisted on showing us. Two hours later we were allowed to reenter the house. Ronnie looked at his sister and asked, "Did you learn?"

Our house in Lake Conway Estates was about three blocks from a community lot on the edge of the lake. Carol and I often took the kids there to play in and around the lake. During one of these outings Alison was playing with a large beach ball that got away from her. The ball started floating towards the center of the lake. I began swimming after it. I had done no extensive swimming for years. As a boy I could swim forever, but on this day I was not in top physical condition. I was out about a hundred yards when suddenly I felt myself getting tired. I let the ball go and started back to the shore. By the time I reached land, I was exhausted. Another hundred yards and I could have drowned.

During one of his last visits to Orlando, I was amused into recognition that Ronnie Roehrich had ceased being a boy and had become a man, Ronald L. Roehrich. He had been graduated from the University of Arkansas. He had joined the Navy and attended flight school in Pensacola. He had completed flight school and received a commission. One evening he said to Carol and me, "I think I'd like to go out to the officer's club," referring to the officer's club at McCoy Air Force base. I was a member of the officer's club. I said, "Sure Ronnie, we'll take you." Standing there in the uniform of a Navy Ensign Ron said to me, "Cecil, I think I can get in by myself."

Lieutenant junior grade Ronald L. Roehrich received orders that would take him to Vietnam.

I received word that my position with the U. S. Army Missile Command was being moved to Huntsville, Alabama. We did not want to move to Huntsville. Cecil Kuehnert, who had been the District Counsel and my supervisor when I worked in Little Rock, told me that there would soon be a vacancy in the Galveston District of the Corps of Engineers, as District Counsel. Mr. Kuehnert was at this time the Division Counsel of the South Atlantic Division, in Atlanta, Georgia. I talked with Carol. We agreed that we might like living in Galveston. It was closer to Dallas, where Carol's brother Bob lived. It would mean a return to working for the U.S. Army Corps of Engineers, the organization I worked for in Little Rock and for which I had great respect. While we waited for the vacancy in Galveston to materialize, I continued to look into other possible options. We had time to make sure we went someplace we wanted to go. The planned reorganization within the Missile Command was still months from implementation.

The last night Ron was with us before he went overseas, he and I went out alone. We talked about his approaching assignment in Vietnam. Ron well understood the dangers that would be confronting him. He would do the best job he could for the Navy, and for the country. He believed that he was well-trained.

Unfortunately, the pilots had not been trained for night flying.

fifteen

Our door bell rang. Carol was home alone. She answered.

Standing in front of the door was a man in the uniform of a Navy officer. Carol was repelled ten feet back into the room. Her mind conjured defenses to the realization of her worst fear. "He's a policeman; Kris has been misbehaving in school," was one possible protection.

The man opened the door and quietly entered our home.

"Mrs. Roehrich?" he asked.

"I'm his sister," Carol said.

"There's been an accident," the man told her.

"Is he dead?" Carol asked.

No words were necessary to convey the answer.

The man came to our home because Ensign Ronald L. Roehrich gave our home to the Navy as his permanent address. His parents were retired and the stability of their location never absolutely certain. On this day Nicholas J. and Grace Roehrich were living in Donna, Texas. Carol told the officer where and how they could be contacted.

Carol called me at the office. I came right home.

That night Carol's parents called us from Texas. Three words of this conversation are indelible in my mind. Carol's father said, "We lost Ron!"

When he was killed, Ronald L. Roehrich was twenty six years, two month and two days old. He was born in Langdon, North Dakota, on November 16, 1941. He died in Vietnam on January 18, 1968. His body was to forever rest in the Gulf of Tonkin.

A few days before Ronnie died, we received a letter from him, written aboard the U. S. S. Kitty Hawk, on the back and front of a yellow, legal size sheet of paper, dated "5 Jan 68." The letter begins with "Hi--." In the body of the letter he wrote:

Congratulations to Cec & his Oklahoma team on their victory over Tennessee. Maybe next year I'll be able to watch the bowl games with you.

I thought Texas A&M made a good showing also. We, of course, didn't get to see the games but we read the news reports. Maybe we will get the films later this month.

I am glad that Kris & Al liked their gifts. Only wish that I could have been there this year again. By the way, are hand-carved walnut salad bowls, etc., considered in good taste? I'm not too hip on which household products are considered chic and which are not. How much is a set of, lets say, 1 large and 5 small wooden bowls in the states? Please inform.

Not too much to say about the war. It is a startling experience to see missiles and flack exploding in the air all around you. I'm not too frightened but my adrenal glands have been working overtime the last couple of days. The day before yesterday I called out a SAM to my pilot and he saw it just in time to jinx and it missed us, thank God. I'm fairly certain it was tracking our aircraft. It exploded overhead after

we had avoided it. This was over Haiphong --
probably the second worst place in N.V., as far
as antiaircraft defenses are concerned. One of
the airplanes that was flying next to us got hit
by a SAM. I didn't see it hit him -- because at the
time I was looking the other way. He was able to
eject though and I believe he is alive, probably
captured. Then again yesterday we went back
to Haiphong so I was quite concerned after my
last experience. However, it wasn't nearly as
bad -- no missiles and medium amount of flack
only. We never even got hit; I mean none of our
planes. Well must run now, cause we're going
again in a couple hours and I have to brief for
the flight.

Will write again soon with the second
chapter in the exciting life of Ronald L., Hero of
Vietnam.

What happened, what I knew about how Ron
was killed, is explained in a letter I wrote to one
of Carol's cousins, Donna M. Wilkie, years later
after both Carol and her father had died. Donna
wrote to me asking questions after she visited a
reproduction of the Vietnam Veteran's Memorial in
Cavalier, North Dakota. "Where did Ronnie go to
college? What did he get a degree in? Do you know
what his job in the Navy was?" I responded to her
letter as follows.

Ronnie graduated from the University of
Arkansas. He was a math major. He decided on
the U. of Arkansas, I believe, because Carol and
I lived in Little Rock at the time he completed
high school, and because the fishing is good in
Arkansas.

He entered the Navy in participation in
an officer training program. He did not train
as a pilot, probably because his eyesight was
less than perfect. Instead, he became what I

simplistically call a "Radio man." He was part of the 2 man team (with the pilot) flying an F-4 fighter jet.

I'm sending you a copy of a letter we received from Ron, not long before he was killed. His plane was not shot down. It was destroyed in an accident, flying at night in apparent total darkness. The plane was flying low, and, as I understand, went too low and hit the water of the sea, Gulf of Tonkin. I'm also sending you a copy of a news report, undated, from the paper in Langdon. I assume they got some information directly from the Navy.

Ronnie's death pretty much destroyed the Roehrich family. None of them -- not Nick, Grace, Bob, Jim or Carol -- ever got over it. Literally, they all became casualties of the Vietnam War. And truthfully, I never got over it either. I'm also sending you a copy of a letter to the editor of some newspaper that Carol clipped and saved. It pretty well tells the story.

I'll tell you of one incident that well illustrates the Roehrich pain. Some twenty years after Ron's death, Nick and Grace were visiting Carol and me in Portland. Nick was working in our back yard when suddenly he started crying, not aloud, sobbing, just tears flowing. My poor son-in-law didn't know what to do, or think. Tactfully, my daughter Alison, who well understood, told her husband Courtney to just leave the old man be.

The news article I sent to Donna was published in the Cavalier County, North Dakota, *Republican* some eight months after he was killed. The article is captioned "Lt. Roehrich Dies On Air Duty in Vietnam Action." It reads:

Circumstances of the death in Vietnam action of Lt. j.g. Ronald Roehrich, 26, native of Langdon, were reported to the Republican this week. Though he was missing in action January 18 and presumed lost on that mission, news of his death did not become available to the Republican until last month.

Veteran of 20 missions from the carrier, U. S. S. Kitty Hawk, Lt. Roehrich and his pilot were sent to investigate an unidentified craft in the Gulf of Tonkin. The mission started in the total darkness before dawn on the morning of January 18 with low overcast and low visibility. Lt. Roehrich reported back to the Kitty Hawk that the craft under surveillance was a friendly cargo type craft and seconds later all contact with his plane was lost. An exhaustive search was conducted, but no survivors were found.

Memorial services were held on board the U. S. S. Kitty Hawk January 23, 1968.

Ronald L. Roehrich was born November 16, 1941, in Langdon, the son of Nick and Grace Roehrich. He was graduated from high school at East Grand Forks and after his graduation from the University of Arkansas in 1965 he enlisted in the U.S. Naval Air Corps. After his training he sailed from San Diego in November, 11 months ago, on the U. S. S. Kitty Hawk for carrier flight duty in the Gulf of Tonkin.

The Roehrich family lived in Langdon from 1933 until 1945 and after that in Perham, Minn., Edgeley, East Grand Forks and other places after Mr. Roehrich retired from business at East Grand Forks.

Lt. Roehrich's parents now reside in San Diego. A sister and two brothers also survive. His sister is Mrs. Cecil (Carol) Reinke, Galveston, Tex., and his brothers are Robert

Roehrich, Dallas, Tex., and James Roehrich, in Missouri.

The "letter to the editor of some newspaper" I referred to in my letter to Donna has found a place among the things Carol kept and I have stored away for our children and grandchildren. It was written by a woman Carol did not know but with whom she shared an unbearable pain. The woman's name is Ruth Sipchen. The woman wrote in a hand guided by undying love for her son who was lost in Vietnam. Her son's name is now forever enshrined on a wall in our nation's capital, as is that of Lt. j.g. Ronald L. Roehrich. What this mother wrote is captioned "Lest we forget, Reflection:"

Almost as though it were yesterday, I can see your solemn little face turned up to mine, your dark hair springing as though in surprise from a head which just fits into the palm of my hand.

You yawn hugely and wind miniature fingers halfway around one of mine, and all the way around my heart. I kiss your hand and wonder dreamily what wondrous things it will one day accomplish. Will it design skyscrapers, build bridges, make world-changing discoveries, hold a child of its own?

As you grew and changed, so did your dreams: First a fireman, then a policeman, next a race car driver, and finally, a lawyer like your dad -- right after you helped settle this Vietnam thing.

Today I searched for your name among the almost 58,000 others carved on a black granite wall in Washington. The moment I found it, I felt the tiny fingers wind again around mine and I traced each of the 12 letters of your name hoping to somehow make contact with you.

Mixed with my pride, my grief and my terrible sense of loss, the still- unanswered question silently screams, "Why?"

We talked of so many wonderful things for you, you and I, hoped so many hopes, but this wall was never -- never once -- among them!

I am not aware of my tears, my very first, until I feel them splash on my clenched hands. I feel the tiny fingers circling mine, at last, slowly, let go.

Over two and one-half million Americans served in Vietnam. 58,169 were killed. 304,000 were wounded. 75,000 suffered injuries that left them severely disabled.

Whenever our country sends men and women to war, whether in Korea, Vietnam, or elsewhere, the question inevitably arises, as casualties increase, "Is the cause worth all those lives?" This is the wrong question. The question that should be asked, before hostilities start, is, "Is this cause worth a single life?" The biggest number is always one.

Carol said to me, "I wish I could tell Ronnie one more time how much I love him." I could only say, "He knows, honey. He knows."

I regret ever having said of Carol's brother Ronnie, "He's an ordinary kid."

This today I would gladly admit to my wife, Ronnie was no ordinary kid.

Three words tell what I think of the Vietnam War. "We lost Ron!"

sixteen

Six months after Lt. j.g. Ronald L. Roehrich died in Vietnam, we moved to Galveston, Texas. Our daughter Kris was ten years old. Our daughter Alison was five. I started in my new job, as the District Counsel for the Galveston District of the U. S. Army Corps of Engineers, on June 2, 1968. I was hopeful that moving to a new location, starting life in a new place, would in someway ease Carol's pain. I believe it did help some. What helped most was that she had two daughters who loved her, and whom she loved. She lived with the pain of losing Ronnie for the rest of her life. Over time, the surges of pain came less often, but they never diminished.

The year 1968 was a damnable year, a year painful to remember.

Our country was being torn apart by the Vietnam War.

Lyndon Johnson was in his last year as president. He seemed a tortured man. Struggle though he might, his hole that was the Vietnam War was now too deep for him to climb out.

On June 8, Senator Robert F. Kennedy was killed, shot by Sirhan Bishara Sirhan just minutes after claiming victory in the California democratic presidential primary.

Two months earlier, on April 6, Dr. Martin Luther King had been fatally shot by James Earl Ray in Memphis, Tennessee.

Three lives -- those of President John F. Kennedy, Dr. Martin Luther King, and Senator Robert F. Kennedy -- are everlastingly linked in American history. Each of these men strived to make the world a better place. They each believed that, as President Kennedy once said, "In this world, God's work is truly our own."

We bought a home on Golfcrest Avenue about four miles from the center of town. Of importance to our daughter Kris, we were soon to learn, the house had a fenced yard.

Serving as the District Counsel for the Galveston District of the U.S. Army Corps of Engineers was for me a satisfying experience. It presented challenging work for a lawyer. It offered my first opportunity to supervise a staff of lawyers and clerical personnel. I welcomed the responsibility. I thought it the best job I could ever want.

Shortly after we arrived, Carol and I with our children were invited to dinner in the home of Mr. and Mrs. Douglas Graham. Doug Graham was Chief of The Engineering Division, the most influential civilian in the Galveston District. Carol was adamant about cleanliness, in our own home and in hotels and motels where we stayed. When traveling by car, we usually stopped at Holiday Inns. Between stops for lodging, we also stopped at Holiday Inns to use the restrooms. The facilities were invariably clean, but even so, Carol always checked. Our children learned to inspect. While we were in the Graham house, Alison used the bathroom. She came out exclaiming, "Oh Mommy, they have a clean potty chair." Thank God Mrs. Graham was a good housekeeper. If she had not been, our little Alison would have said so.

When we moved to Galveston, we were still a one-car family. I had always been able to carpool to work, so Carol had the car most of the time. I tried to continue carpooling. Four engineers that worked for the Galveston District lived on our street. I called every one of them, "Would you like to carpool to work?" From each of them I heard the same thing, drawled out in a Texas accent, "I like to drive my own car."

Kris would be going into the fifth grade. Alison would be starting Kindergarten. Island Elementary School, which both our children would be attending, was located only a few blocks from our house. The distance would have been walkable except for one thing. To get to the school from our house you had to cross Stewart Road, a quite busy street. Both Carol and I well understood that the kids, Alison for sure, would have to be driven to school. The day before school was to start I was sitting in my office, knowing I would have to do something. Across the street was a Rambler dealer. I walked across. On the showroom floor was a blue, 1968 Rambler hardtop convertible. I bought it. It was the best car we ever owned. We were a two-car family from that day forward.

Three things can be learned from my experiences while working in Galveston. It pays to be honest. Rudeness is to be avoided; politeness embraced. And, if you want minorities to apply for a job, you must first convince them that there is a job.

Let me tell a story, a story about an honest man. The man's name was King Fisher. Mr. Fisher owned a dredging company in Texas. His company did a lot of work for the Galveston District of the Corps of Engineers. When I first met him, shortly after I started work as the District Counsel, his company had a substantial claim against the Corps. I analyzed his claim. Unfortunately for Mr. Fisher and his company, I found the claim to be without merit. His claim was denied, and the denial was appealed to the Corps of Engineers Board of Contract Appeals.

During the hearing before the Board, at which I represented the Corps, Mr. Fisher was a witness for his company. On cross-examination, I asked him a number of questions about conditions encountered during his company's dredging operation, questions that I knew if answered honestly would defeat his company's claim. Mr. Fisher was not a stupid man. To the contrary, while without extensive formal education, he was a very bright man, intelligent enough and capable enough to build a substantial dredging company. He knew what he could say to deflect my questions and support his company's claim. What did I hear from Mr. Fisher? The truth, the whole truth, and nothing but the truth! He did not, would not, and likely could not lie. The direct result, his company lost before the Board of Contract Appeals. The claim was held to be without merit; his company received no increased compensation. An attendant result, after that day I never questioned that when Mr. Fisher was telling me something, right or wrong, he was telling me what he believed to be the absolute truth.

I was the District Counsel for the Galveston District for ten years. Mr. Fisher's company continued to do work for the Corps. From time to time the company had claims. On occasions, Mr. Fisher would personally talk with me and other representatives of the Corps, telling what had occurred. My common response, if Mr. Fisher says that's what happened, that's very likely what happened. Let's check it out, of course, but know this: Mr. Fisher does not lie.

Ironically, Mr. Fisher lost the one case we tried. But over the years, he made money, and saved the Corps a lot of money because I knew he was honest.

Let me tell another story, a story about two lawyers.

One lawyer was an elderly gentleman with silver gray hair. He visited in conference with me and the District Commander. He had with him a client, a contractor with a claim against the Corps of Engineers. He was very polite. He said things like, "Colonel, we appreciate that the Corps has always been very fair to us. We hate being in here with a claim. But we must in this case respectfully request a fair settlement. Simply put, unless you can recognize the merit of our claim, our company will lose a lot of money. We can't afford that, and I don't believe the Corps can either." Upon finishing his explanation of the claim, he took his leave, shaking hands with the Colonel and me, and saying something like, "We will appreciate your consideration of our claim. And thanks for listening."

After this lawyer was gone, and the District Commander and I were left to ourselves, the Colonel looked to me and said, "Cecil, see what you can do for the guy."

The other attorney was much younger. He too brought along a client with a claim against the Corps. He was rude as hell. He said things like, "We're tired of the arrogance of the Corps of Engineers. Your Project Engineer thinks he's God on a stick. The Corps screwed up, and now you people are trying to cheat us. We've got a good claim and you damn well better pay it." The Colonel listened and I listened. When this attorney was finished, he too shook hands as he took his leave, but he left threatening, "Remember, if we have to, we'll go to court on this thing. You owe us, and we damn well intend to collect."

When this attorney left, the Colonel and I sat for awhile, digesting what was said. I thought of him, some attorneys would rather impress their clients than help them. Disgusted, the Colonel turned to me and pronounced, "Cecil, you give that 'Son of a Bitch' one dime and you're fired."

Of course I wasn't going to be fired. I would look at his claim, and if it had merit it would be paid. Still, as Lyndon Johnson often said, "Some guys are hard to help."

I have yet a third story.

I had become increasingly concerned that despite the long standing Federal policy mandating fair consideration of minority applicants for employment, the Galveston District of the Corps of Engineers, including the Office of Counsel, my office, was still an almost lily-white organization. My office, consisting of five lawyers and three clerical personnel, had only one Hispanic employee, no black employees. I had an opportunity to hire a law student for the summer, to clerk in my office. I wanted to remedy this disparate situation, at least temporarily, by hiring a minority law student.

As an employee of the Government, with selection authority, it was within my discretion to decide to which law schools I would send the notice that we would be hiring a summer law clerk. Confident that I would find good candidates, I decided to send the notice to one law school, and one law school only, the Texas Southern University School of Law in Houston. Texas Southern is a historically black school, with an integrated student body. I knew this university had a good law school. I had met and had discussions with the dean, Mr. Otis King.

After sending out the notice that my office would be hiring a law student for the summer, I talked on the telephone with a Mr. Johnson, the faculty member in charge of helping students find summer employment. We agreed on a time when I would come to the school to conduct interviews. The day came. At eight in the morning I was in the interview room. With me to help conduct the interviews was Mr. Tom J. Smith, Jr., the Equal Employment Opportunity Officer for the Galveston District. We sat in the interview room for two hours. Not one student showed up to be interviewed.

We left the interview room and walked into the offices of the law school dean.

In the dean's offices was a professor who taught contract law. The man asked me what we were doing there, what we wanted. I explained that we had come to conduct interviews; that we were interested in hiring a law student to clerk for the summer. I told him that we had sat in the interview room for two hours, but that it looked like we would be going home empty handed. Apparently none of the students was interested.

The professor challenged me, "Look, these kids aren't stupid. They don't like being used. They know that you'll come here, make a good show of pretending to be an equal opportunity employer. Then you'll go back to your office and hire some student from Southern Methodist or the University of Texas."

I informed the man, "I sent the announcement of this job to only one school, this law school. I'm either going to hire a student from this school, or I'm not going to hire anyone at all."

"Is that true?" he questioned.

"Yes sir," I assured him, "that's a fact."

He said to me, with authority, "You go back into that interview room."

Mr. Smith and I returned to the interview room.

The professor told his class that this was a real job opportunity, that I had said I was going to hire someone from the Texas Southern University School of Law.

Within twenty minutes a student came in to be interviewed, then another, and another, and another. Literally, I believe we interviewed every student in the law school. Mr. Smith and I were in the interview room from ten-thirty in the morning until after ten at night.

I hired a student from this law school. He proved to be a brilliant law clerk. The next spring I asked the District Commander for a personnel space so I could hire him full time. The Colonel was every bit as interested in trying to hire minorities as I was, maybe more so. He approved my request. I offered the young man a permanent position. Unfortunately for me, he could not accept. Otis King had become the City Attorney for Houston. The young man was hired by his former law school dean.

Like I said, if you want minorities to apply for a job, you must first convince them that there is a job. Like the professor said, "They don't like being used."

Incidentally, the law school at Texas Southern University is now "The Thurgood Marshall School of Law."

seventeen

We found in Galveston the world's best neighbors. Across the street was the home of Charles and Leah Rosenbloom and their daughter Judy, who was a few years older than Kris. Also on that side of the street were Dr. and Mrs. Zein-Eldin, Ahmed and Zoula. On our side of the street lived John and Grace Kay and their three children, Ross, Janet Elizabeth, and Bradford K. Kay. Adjacent to our house was the home of the Katz family. The Katz family consisted of Max and Ruth, their two sons Neil and Steven, their daughter Anita, and Ruth's widowed mother Sarah, Mrs. Abraham Goldberg, a woman in her upper eighties.

During our third year of living on Golfcrest, our neighborhood was enhanced by the addition of the family of K. Ball and Anne Withers. They moved onto our side of the street. K. Ball and Anne had two daughters named Susan and Pamela. Not long afterwards, our neighborhood was further enhanced by the coming of two families. Dr. and Mrs. Leo J. Castiglioni, "Cass" and Lois, moved onto our side of the street. They had two children, their son Donald and daughter Kay. Robert and Marjorie Brotman, Bob and Margie, bought a house across the street. The Brotmans had two sons, David and Ira.

Max Katz had a scrap metal business, apparently a quite good one. The Katz family lived in the largest house on our street. It had separate mother-in-law quarters.

One day when I left our home for my office, I somehow locked Carol out of our house. Carol went to the Katz house, and Mrs. Goldberg let her in to use the telephone. She called me and I came home. The next day I did the same thing, locked Carol out of our house. Again Carol went to the Katz house and again Mrs. Goldberg let her use the phone. This time Carol was upset, really angry with "that man." Mrs. Goldberg said to Carol, "It doesn't do any good to get mad." Recalling her own deceased husband she reminisced, "What you gonna do? Fifty years I lived with that man. Every day aggravation. Ten years he's been gone. Every day I miss the aggravation." Amused, Carol couldn't wait to tell me what Mrs. Goldberg had said. I was no longer in trouble.

Charlie Rosenbloom was the Director of the Department of Social Services of the University of Texas Medical Branch at Galveston. He was a remarkable man, extremely bright, knew almost everything one man can know about art, literature, and music. As a Captain in the Army during World War II, he was one of the first Americans to see the horrors of Dachau. It was an experience he never talked about. How that horrifying sight affected him I don't know. I do know this. He was the one of the finest men, the most charitable man, I have ever known. Perhaps as much as anyone within my experience, he understood what is not important in life, and what is important.

Dr. Zein-Eldin had a Ph.D. in chemistry. He had been a professor at the University of Texas Medical Branch at Galveston. Early on he saw that his students almost immediately after completion of their studies earned twice or more the amount of money that he did. He erased the disparity by going to medical school himself. He became a very successful psychiatrist. He was always most proud, however, of having earned a Ph.D. in chemistry.

John Kay was a lawyer. He worked for the First Hutchings-Sealy National Bank in Galveston.

Grace Kay, sometimes called "Jog," was a very talented woman. She could tell funny stories, self-deprecating humor. She was also a very astute observer of the human condition. She told us what she saw when she and John went to New York to attend a national banker's convention. What she said has forever affected the way I greet new acquaintances, what I say about myself when introduced to someone for the first time.

When in New York for the national banker's convention, she noticed that whenever she and John were introduced to someone, that person invariably told them not only his name, but also his title or position. "Hello, I'm John Doe. I'm President of The First National Bank of Podunk." It was as if that person wanted them to know up front that they were meeting someone important. It was safer than risking being judged on his or her personal merit.

Before marrying, Mrs. Kay worked as a private secretary for George P. Mitchell, one of the richest oil men in Texas. One day her employer gave her fifty dollars "to buy a hat." Later the man offered to see the hat. She said, "I didn't buy a hat, I bought a car." Mr. Mitchell's response, "Let's go. I've got to see the car you can buy for fifty dollars."

She answered the front doorbell of her house. It was two young men from the Jehovah Witnesses religion, proselytizing. "Do you want to go through eternity in heaven?" one of the two asked. "Oh honey," she answered, "I'm having such a hard time getting through this life, I just can't think about what I'll do after."

K. Ball Withers was a lawyer. He was a Harvard law school graduate. He had a private practice in Galveston. I thought K. Ball to be an exceptionally fine lawyer. Talking with him, I was always reminded of how my law school roommate, Mike Nilles, distinguished between an attorney and a lawyer. Mike said, "An attorney is someone admitted to practice. A lawyer is someone who knows the law."

K. Ball's interests extended beyond the law. He was passionate about community theatre. He liked to direct plays, and he was good at it. His wife, Anne, was an excellent actor, with talent I thought could have succeeded on Broadway.

Carol was an excellent seamstress. She made most of her own clothes and almost all of the dresses our children wore. She made me a sports coat that I still keep although I am long since too heavy to wear it. Our home was inundated with sewing equipment.

At age three our little Kris asked her mother, "When I go to college, will you make me dresses that button down the front, so I can dress myself?"

K. Ball wanted to produce and direct "The Lion in Winter," a play written by James Goldman. He had one problem. Rental of the costumes was too expensive. He knew Carol could sew almost anything. He came to our house and asked Carol if she would make the costumes. Carol made every costume, including the shoes. Anne Withers starred in the play, in the role of Eleanor of Aquitaine, made famous on film by Katherine Hepburn. After the run of the play, the local community theatre group rented the costumes to other amateur theatre organizations.

Another time, K. Ball was to produce and direct the Noel Coward play "Hay Fever." Anne would star in the role of Judith Bliss. He again came to our house. This time he did not want Carol to make costumes. He wanted our daughter Kris, then a high school student, to play Sorel Bliss, the daughter of Judith and David. Kris had no particular interest in acting, but she accepted. The play was performed six evenings, Monday through Saturday, on the stage in the American National Insurance Company building in Galveston. I attended every performance but one. Kris thought enough was enough. Before her last performance, she told me to stay home.

Alison liked going to school. She did good school work. She interacted well with her peers. After school and on weekends, our house was filled with her friends. Carol and I were delighted. With this child we had no school related worries.

We learned some things from our children, things parents ought to know.

Alison was a very gregarious kid. She always had friends tramping through the house. They were always welcome. Carol was a stay-at-home mother. She liked her children at home, with whatever friends they wanted. But one thing Alison did always tended to upset us. She would come up to Carol or me, or both of us, with a little friend in hand and ask, can so and so stay for dinner? We would say to Alison, when we got a private moment, "Don't bring your friends with you to ask if they can stay for dinner. Come see us alone and ask. That way, if for any reason your friends can't stay, we won't hurt their feelings by saying no." Kris told us that we, not Alison, did not understand what was proper in this situation. She explained that children don't care whether you say yes or no to the question of whether they can stay for dinner. "They don't get hurt feelings, whatever the answer. They just want to know."

When Alison was in the fourth grade, she liked playing softball with the other kids. One thing never seen in our family is athletic talent. I played three years of high school football, if you count sitting on the bench as playing. When we played Trivial Pursuit, Carol and Kris thought they should get credit for the sports questions if they could identify the sport to which the question related. Carol asked Alison, "Are you good at playing softball?" Alison answered, "No, but I'm good at talking it up."

Except for Alison, we were a family without musical talent. Carol sang in our college choir, but she was never in danger of being asked to perform as a soloist. Alison could sing like a bird. One day, while cleaning house and listening to the radio, Carol was astonished by what she heard. What she heard was Alison singing on the radio. Island Elementary School was running a campaign to raise money to air-condition the school classrooms, and, unbeknown to us, our Little Red Alison's voice was chosen to sing the campaign jingle.

Carol's children were raised to be without racial prejudice.

When Alison was in the first grade at Island Elementary, I came to pick her up after school. I found her playing on the jungle bars. I said to her, "Honey, it's time to go home." She said, "I don't want to go home now. I'm playing with the boy in the red coat." I looked over to where she had been playing. The boy was wearing a red coat.

When Alison was in the eighth grade, to enhance integration, the Galveston school board combined all eighth grades in one school. All eighth graders were put in the building that earlier housed Central High School. Central High had been a school for African-American students. Alison was bussed to the school. This was more than just okay with Carol and me. We were very much in favor of integrating the schools. Occasionally, Carol or I would drive her. Once when Carol let Alison out of our car, she saw a black boy jump in front of Alison. For almost a second she thought, oh no, a racial confrontation. Then she saw that it was something entirely different. The boy was a friend, congratulating Alison on having the braces removed from her teeth.

While we were living in Galveston, a new college opened only twenty miles from our home, The University of Houston at Clear Lake City. Evening classes were offered. Carol and I took advantage of the opportunity to attend graduate school. Carol earned a Master of Humanities.

I received a Master's degree in Environmental Management.

Attending with us was Charlotte Hough, the wife of Bill Hough, one the lawyers that worked with me in the Office of Counsel. Charlotte Hough was the most beautiful woman I have ever seen, Hollywood beauties notwithstanding. One evening another lawyer from my office, David Talton, called our home looking for me. Carol told him I was not at home, that Charlotte Hough and I had driven to Clear Lake City to attend classes. She said to David, to his great amusement, "You must admit, when I send my husband out with another woman, I send him with nothing but the very best."

Alison's kindergarten teacher was Charlotte Ray. Mrs. Ray was the wife of Dr. Sammy Ray, a marine biologist. Dr. Ray was a professor at Texas A&M University at Galveston. We did not know at this time how valuable a role Dr. and Mrs. Ray were to play in the education of our children. Mrs. Ray started the education of Alison. Together, they would give us invaluable advice on how to educate Kris.

The Rays understood bright children. They had one, their daughter Judy. When kids started school in Galveston, it was the policy of the educators to interview each one, to better understand their background. The Ray's daughter was interviewed. One of the things the woman who talked with her asked was, "Do you know what a toothbrush is?" The Ray girl came from her interview and said to her mother, "Can you imagine that? A grown woman asked me, a child, what a toothbrush was. Disgusting!"

eighteen

We had been in Galveston only a short while when Kris approached her mother carrying a newspaper advertisement. A family living not far from us had poodle puppies for sale. Kris "reminded" her mother, "You said that if we had a fenced yard we could get a dog." Carol and I had never talked about or thought about getting a dog. Likely, while we were living in Orlando in a house without a fence, Kris had said she wanted a dog and Carol had said we couldn't have a dog because we didn't have a fenced yard.

Carol said, "Okay, we will go look at the puppies."

Carol, Kris, and Alison visited the family with the puppies. There were only two left, housed in a cardboard box, a little black one, a female, and a little apricot one, a male. The little black puppy was being very quiet. The little male poodle was jumping all around the box. While they were looking at the puppies, Alison picked up the little black dog. Carol said, pointing to the apricot, "We'll take this one." Alison, suddenly realizing they were not just looking, dropped the little black dog back into the box and grabbed the one selected by the neck all in one motion, screaming with new found incredulity and red-headed joy, "We gonna take this puppy dog home?"

Carol told me later, "Alison grabbed the little dog by the neck and didn't let go. We're lucky she didn't choke the little fellow, but at least he knew he was wanted."

On the way home, Kris asked to stop at the local drugstore. They had a dog collar that Kris liked, one with lots of rhinestones. For days, when walking home from school, Kris had been stopping to look at the collar. Each day she moved it to the back as if that would keep someone else from buying it. Carol stopped. Kris went in and bought the collar.

I did not know we were getting a dog until after the fact when I called home from my office. While talking with Carol, I could hear Alison yelling joyously in the background. According to Carol the volume didn't go down for hours.

Alison invited all the neighborhood kids to "play with her dog." One of the boys complained to Carol, "Alison's idea of playing with her dog is we all stand and watch while she holds it."

Kris named the dog Sir Frederick of Golfcrest. We called him Fred, or Freddie.

We took Fred to a veterinarian, Dr. Sid Kay. Dr. Kay was a very brilliant man. He would have gone to medical school were his religion not Judaism. In his day the medical schools still had quotas, only so many Jews allowed. The irony of this is that, when we lived in Texas, it was harder to get into the veterinary school at Texas A&M than it was to get into medical school at the University of Texas. We knew a young man who went to medical school because he couldn't get into veterinary school. Sid Kay questioned how this could come to be, "Haven't we got our priorities straight?"

In front of us, when we first visited Dr. Kay, was a woman with a dog. We could hear the veterinarian say to the woman, "This dog is a puppy. Take it home and love it." I don't know anything about the condition of the dog. I just know that is what Dr. Kay said, "Take it home and love it." Then he gets to us. Our two kids, of course, are carrying our new poodle puppy. Dr. Kay takes one look at Fred and says, "You're all worn out."

I remember when and how Freddie became Carol's dog.

We had in our house in Galveston what we call the red boxes, wood boxes three feet by one and a half in surface size, two feet in depth. I still have these boxes in our Portland home. When Lt. j.g. Ronald L. Roehrich was killed, the Navy shipped his personal effects home in these boxes. Carol did not want to destroy the boxes; they were too much a part of Ronnie. I painted the boxes red. We put them in Carol's sewing room, placed end to end with a small gap between. Carol used the boxes to store material. One day Freddie evidently tried walking between the two boxes. He got stuck. He could not get out. When Carol found him, he was a little puppy in distress. She rescued him. They bonded. She saw the vulnerability of a little puppy. He saw her as his savior. From that moment on he was Carol's dog. The rest of us came second. When we would come home from an outing, Fred would run past me and the children to greet Carol; then he'd come back and greet the rest of us, in no particular order.

We knew nothing about training a dog. We didn't need to know how to house train him. Freddie trained himself. He never made a mess in our home. He had too much class. He was a gentleman.

Knowing nothing about training a dog, we made one major mistake. Like any little boy, Fred had a sense of adventure. Our back yard was never a world big enough for him. If we left the gate open and he could get out, Freddie was gone. The first time he experienced adventure we got in our car and drove around until we found him. We picked him up and brought him home. The next few times he got out we repeated this mistake. Freddie quickly learned that when he was ready to go home all he had to do was sit down on the nearest corner and wait for us to come and get him. Every time the dog disappeared we had to get in our car and go looking until we found the great adventurer.

One day Carol and I were out in our back yard. Fred was in the yard with us, running around. For some reason the gate was open. Freddie was not even sniffing near the gate. "Look at him," Carol said to me. "Innocence personified. He wouldn't even think about going out that gate." Then she said, "Let me show you something." We went in the back of the house and ran out the front door. We intercepted the devious little creature, outside the gate, making his way to the street.

Freddie was about three years old when the Brotman family bought a house across the street. They were just moving in; we had not met them yet when Fred made one of his escapes. Carol stepped into our front yard and saw the little fluff running down the street. "Fred," she called, loud as a fishwife, "you get back here. You get back here right now. If you don't get back here right now, you're in big trouble." Mrs. Brotman heard Carol screaming at Fred, only she didn't know Fred was a dog. She went back into her house and, as she later told us, said to her husband Bob, "Did you hear how that woman talks to her husband?"

Bob and Marge Brotman had two boys, David and Ira. They were the cutest kids in town. They were so cute that, literally twenty years later, after they were both grown, professional men, the Galveston newspaper was still running pictures of the Brotman boys, as children.

David used to come to our house every day at four o'clock to watch an adventure program for children, entitled "Sky King" or something similar, on our television set. Why he chose to come to our house I don't know. I'm certain his home had television. Perhaps he liked visiting. We didn't care. He was welcome.

One of the funniest things I ever saw involved Ira Brotman, age about three, in our house trying to protect a small bag of cookies from Fred. Ira was heading toward Alison's room and had to pass by our family room davenport. Freddie was on the davenport, paws on the arm, leaning over little Ira crouched like a vulture. There was little Ira, holding his cookies away from Fred as best he could decrying, "No, Gaug! No, Gaug!"

A story follows Alison's six-year-old birthday party. One little girl goes home. Her mother asks her, "How was the party?" "It was fun," she exclaimed, "except for that Fred. They should have thrown Fred out. They should have thrown Fred right out of there. He shouldn't have been invited." The mother said to her child, as the story came to us, "That's not a nice way to talk about a little boy." To which the child replied, "Mother, Fred's not a little boy. He's a little dog."

Freddie followed Carol everywhere. If she was in the kitchen, he was in the kitchen. If she was in her sewing room, he was in the sewing room. When she was cleaning the house, he followed her room to room. His devotion reminded me of the poem, "My Shadow," by Robert Louis Stevenson:

I have a little shadow that goes in and out with me,

And what can be the use of him is more than I can see.

We noticed that every time Carol left the house, left Fred home alone, when she returned something in the house would be disturbed. Dr. Kay explained. "He's punishing you. It's his way of saying, 'I don't have to put up with this.'" His punishments were never very severe; he would move pillows or disarrange something else in the house. One time Carol stepped out into our garage for no more than a minute. When she returned to the kitchen, he was already punishing her.

The tablecloth was being pulled. "Freddie," she chastened her dog, "this is too much!"

Our family talked about what a great dog Freddie was to the point where half of Galveston came to believe that the Reinkes had this great dog. The people who sold him to us heard how happy we were. They came to our house to see him.

Carol's parents visited us in Texas shortly after Ronnie was killed. While they were visiting, Carol's mother would do some sewing. Fred would sit right beside her. She said to Carol, almost in tears, "He's such good company."

Carol said to her father, "Freddie is a real smart dog." Her father's response, "Coming out of this house, I'd be surprised if he was anything else."

When we traveled on visits or vacation outings, we always took Freddie with us. He stayed with us in hotel and motel rooms. He never made a mess.

We drove from Galveston, Texas to San Diego, California, to visit Carol's parents. We usually stayed in Holiday Inns; they were clean and reliable, and they all had swimming pools. We were looking for a motel. There was no Holiday Inn in sight. We saw what looked like a good motel. It had a sign, "Kennels for Dogs." Carol and I were thinking about stopping. Alison objected. "I'm not staying in any hotel that puts dogs in kennels."

We stopped at the White Sands National Monument in New Mexico. Freddie felt the hot sand on his paws and jumped right back into the car. He wouldn't get out again.

Mr. Melvin Jones was our mailman. He was the best thought-of postal carrier in Galveston. Every family wanted Mr. Jones for their mailman. I remember Carol telling me that she talked to another woman at some social function who complained that Mr. Jones used to be her mailman until they changed his route. Carol talked one time about Mr. Jones to another mailman, who said of the post office managers, "They can't find enough awards to give to Mr. Jones."

Our mailbox was located adjacent to our front door. To get to our mailbox, Mr. Jones had to walk past a large picture window fronting our living room. Fred liked to position himself on one of two large chairs in our living room, very close to the picture window, so he could look out. Mr. Jones obviously thought Fred was cute. When he came to our house, he would rap on the window in front of Fred. Freddie would bark his head off. It became a daily ritual. Mr. Jones would rap the window at Freddie, and Freddie would bark at Mr. Jones. It became their unique game, one they both enjoyed.

One day Mr. Jones had to bring something inside the house. Carol said, "I couldn't tell who was the most scared, Freddie or Mr. Jones." They were paying the price for rapping and barking at each other.

Our house backed up to the Galveston city golf course. The golfers with some regularity sliced balls into our yard. One day a golfer climbed our fence, seeking to retrieve his ball. Carol looked out and saw Freddie barking like mad and the golfer poking at Fred with a golf club. Out she came, screaming at the man, "Don't you touch my dog." The poor fellow had to scramble back over the fence, Fred barking and Carol yelling, obviously a ridiculous sight. Never had anyone paid so dearly for a golf ball.

One time Freddie was very sick. We couldn't get Dr. Kay. Carol said, "I'm going to go over and get Dr. Zein-Eldin." Dr. Zein-Eldin was the psychiatrist who lived across the street. I said, "You can't go across the street and ask Dr. Zein-Eldin to take care of our dog. His profession is not taking care of dogs." She said, "I'm not going to ask him as a doctor. I'll ask him as a fellow dog owner." The psychiatrist came to our house and gave care to Fred.

Only one time did Dr. Kay have to perform surgery on our Fred, a minor operation. "I always like to operate on Fred on Fridays," the veterinarian said, as if our dog were a periodic surgery patient. Carol bit, "Why Fridays?" "Because that way your whole family will have the weekend to nurse him back to health."

On a Veterans Day following Ron's death, Carol and I were both feeling down. Alison provided some relief. She heard us talking about the day. "This is Veterans Day?" she surmised. "Isn't it nice that they have a day for dogs and their doctors."

Freddie was attentive to what was going on. He was always alert.

There was the time I heard our dog barking up a storm at our front window. I looked out and saw a nutty neighbor chasing someone down the street, waving a gun. As I later learned, the person being chased had broken into our neighbor's garage and stolen a few pounds of beef from his freezer, which he promptly dropped upon being pursued. The apparently inept burglar ran onto the golf course behind our house with our neighbor still right behind him, still waving the gun. I think I heard two shots. I was thankful that our neighbor didn't hit the man. Had he done so, he likely would have gone to jail. You may be allowed to kill to protect your home, but once a burglar has left and is running away, you can't chase after him and shoot him. A life is worth more than a few pounds of beef.

One night Fred almost bit me trying to protect Alison. Quite early that evening our little red-head had gone to sleep in the master bedroom. Without turning on the lights, I entered the room to pick up the child and carry her to her own bed. The dog obviously saw me as an intruder and himself as her protector. He vaulted across the room, aiming for my ankle. Only at the last second did he recognize me as her father. Carol said to me, "Next time make some noise. You almost got it."

Dogs are like kids; when they know they are loved, they become sassy and demanding. One day

Carol was in the kitchen making cookies. Fred had the scent. He wanted a cookie. Carol reached for and gave him a dog biscuit. That was clearly not what he wanted. "Pooh," he went, and spit out the biscuit. What he wanted was a homemade cookie, and only a homemade cookie. Like I said, sassy and demanding.

Fred was a really remarkable dog. The interesting thing is, he was a mutt. He did not possess all the refinements of a well-bred poodle. We were often to say of our mutt, "Freddie will never win a dog show. How could he? He doesn't own a dog."

One time Carol was reading a book about poodles, what they should look like, written by two overweight ladies pictured on the cover. "Well Fred," she said to the dog, "you're not perfect, but the two ladies who wrote this book aren't so perfect either."

Freddie was never a possession. He was a member of our family. Our daughters thought of him like a "little brother." Kids are sometimes reluctant to accomplish chores assigned to them, and our kids were no different. Neither of them ever complained when asked to do something for Fred. Whatever they could do for Freddie was immediately done. He was a happy dog. His tail wagged constantly. He loved hearing "Nice boy, good boy, fine boy." Carol and I said of Freddie's own view of his position in the family, "Fred knows he's a dog. He just thinks the word dog means favorite child."

Dogs and people have this in common. They both have a limitless capacity for love, for the love of each other.

Carol said, "I wish Ron could see my dog." I almost cried.

nineteen

Kris was pretty much of a loner, but never lonely. She liked to sit in her room and read her books. I remember as a child hearing that Franklin Delano Roosevelt read six books a week. I didn't believe it. Watching Kris, I came to believe that he did.

She became more and more disenchanted with school. One day a neighbor saw Kris coming home from school carrying a stack of books. "Are those for homework?" our neighbor asked. "No," Kris replied. "They waste enough of my time during the day. I'm not going to let them waste my time at night."

Carol always worried about Kris in school. I never did. When you're a lawyer and you have a ten year old child who can read better than you can, you see very little reason to worry about that child's education.

One teacher said to her, "Kris, you're never going to know anything except what you read in all those books."

At the end of Kris' year in the seventh grade, Carol received what for her was a very disturbing telephone call from Kris' teacher.

"I'm sorry," the woman said, after some preliminaries, "but I'm going to have to fail Kris.

119

She has not done the work she needed to do to pass the seventh grade."

"Well," Carol concluded, "I guess we will have to send her to summer school."

"If you do send her to summer school," the teacher told the mother, "she can't take seventh grade subjects."

"Why not?"

"Because she already knows the seventh grade."

We enrolled Kris in eighth grade summer school at the San Marcos Baptist Academy. The San Marcos Baptist Academy is a boarding school in San Marcos, Texas, a small city about two hundred miles west of Galveston. Kris attended there for six weeks.

When school started the next year, the educators in Galveston put Kris in the ninth grade. Our kid had flunked the seventh grade, attended only six weeks of eighth grade studies, and now she was in high school. Unbelievable? Not to me. Carol was perplexed, but proud. We both hoped Kris might better like going to high school.

On Saint Valentine's Day when Kris was a sophomore, there was delivered to our house a bouquet of flowers sent to her by some boy. Carol asked her, "Who sent these?" Kris responded inattentively, "I don't know." Her mother said to her, "You better find out because you'll have to send a thank you card." The next year, when Kris was a junior, there came to our house another bouquet of flowers, this time with a card identifying the sender. Kris showed no interest. Alison asked her mother, "Why do boys keep sending Kris flowers?" Carol answered, "I don't know; maybe boys just like girls that are hard to get." Wistfully, the little sister said to her mother, "Oh I wish I was hard-to-get."

I recall Kris having only one date while in high school. It was a date for the Junior-Senior prom. She went with a friend of hers, a boy I will call Elmer Edwards. Elmer was a young man forced to live in a wheelchair. He had Muscular Dystrophy. The boy's mother drove them to the prom in a van equipped to hold a wheelchair. Kris wore a royal blue jersey dress with white satin collar and cuffs and a pleated skirt. She was wearing a pearl necklace. The boy brought her a corsage with red roses and green ribbon. Carol and I were proud of our daughter. Elmer's mother was elated. Her son was escorting what I'm sure she thought was a beautiful girl. In my image, that night, our daughter Kris was the prettiest high school girl I had ever seen.

Among Kris' good friends in high school was a young black boy who was a very good student. One day a group of black students was taunting him about being an Oreo, black on the outside, white on the inside. Kris said to the taunters, "Before you criticize someone for being an Oreo, you better give some thought to how much money Nabisco makes."

Near the end of her junior year, Kris came home from school and said to her mother, "I have wonderful news, and good news." I can't recall what Carol said was the wonderful news. The good news was that Kris had earned the highest score in Ball High School on the Preliminary Scholastic Aptitude Test. A few days later the "good news" was published in the newspaper, the Galveston Daily News:

> Twenty-two Galveston County high school seniors have been named as semifinalists in the Merit Scholarship Program of the National Merit Scholarship Corp.
>
> They are among approximately 15,000 semifinalists selected from more than a million students throughout the United States who took the Preliminary Scholastic Aptitude Test.
>
> The Galveston County students, listed by city according to alphabetical order, are:

From Galveston—James L. Hilton, Keryl Kris Reinke and William P. Worzel of Ball High School and Jacquelyn M. Tramonte of O'Connell High School.

The students, reported to be seniors, were actually juniors in high school.

As the school year ended, one boy, obviously a classmate, said to Kris, "It was a pleasure sitting next to those legs."

That summer Kris took two courses at Galveston College, a junior college about two blocks from Ball High School. She earned eight semester hour credits in Chemistry.

Come fall, when it was time for Kris to register for her senior year at Ball High School, the principal insisted that she had to take high school chemistry. Carol went to see the principal. My wife pleaded, "You can't put her in high school chemistry. She'll flunk. She has eight hours of college chemistry." The principal was adamant.

By good fortune, Carol mentioned our dilemma to Charlotte Ray. Mrs. Ray talked to her husband, Dr. Sammy Ray. She called Carol and suggested, "Why don't you just put her in college." Carol acknowledged that she had read about special college programs for bright children, one at the University of Wisconsin. Kris was barely sixteen years old. We would not feel comfortable sending her far from home. Mrs. Ray asked, "How about Galveston junior college?"

I was a Reserve Instructor at Galveston College. I taught business law.

I called the college Registrar, Mr. Michael D. Allen. I said to him, "Mike, I want to come talk with you about registering my daughter Kris to attend Galveston College." Mr. Allen asked, "Cecil, what do I need you for?"

Kris went by herself. She registered. She was now a college student.

Kris loved going to Galveston College. She still thinks of it as "My school."

Kris fitted in well. She drew cartoons for the college newspaper, the "Barometer." She made the President's List. Her second year she was elected Vice-President of the student body. She was nominated by the faculty and administration of the college and selected for listing in "Who's Who" in American junior colleges.

She graduated from Galveston College, with an Associate Arts degree, on May 13, 1976.

She spent the following summer studying at Birkbeck College, staying at Ramsey Hall, University of London.

She attended the University of Tulsa, where she majored in English Literature. She was graduated with a Bachelor of Arts degree on December 16, 1977.

She was nineteen years old.

twenty

After more than ten years in Galveston, we moved to Portland, Oregon. I became the Division Counsel for the North Pacific Division, later the Northwestern Division, of the U. S. Army Corps of Engineers. Kris was twenty-one. She had graduated from college and spent one year teaching the fourth grade. Alison was sixteen and would be a junior in high school. Our little poodle, Sir Fredrick of Golfcrest, was now ten years old.

I reported to work on Tuesday, January 2, 1979.

James Earl "Jimmy" Carter was the President of the United States.

Four months later, Margaret Thatcher of Great Britain became Europe's first woman Prime Minister

Three months earlier Karol Cardinal Wojtyla, Archbishop of Krakow, was elected to the papacy, becoming the first non-Italian leader of the Catholic Church in over four centuries. A native of Poland, the new pope chose to be designated John Paul II.

Six years earlier the war in Vietnam had come to an end.

An Army officer, Lieutenant Colonel William Nolte, reportedly was the last American killed in

Vietnam. Speaking for her husband, the Colonel's wife Joyce said solemnly, "The war has ended. That's all he wanted." His wife knew that Colonel Nolte possessed a deep, unselfish understanding of the tragedy that is war. In a letter to her shortly before his death, the Colonel wrote:

> We tend to think only in terms of what this war has cost us, but by comparison to what it has cost so many Vietnamese, our price pales.

We bought a house on Terwilliger Boulevard. Again, we had a house with a fenced yard. This fence was less necessary than the one in Galveston. Freddie had lost much of his sense of adventure. He was content staying inside the house, always next to Carol.

We were again fortunate in that we inherited good neighbors.

In a house adjacent to ours lived Elmer and Marge Arp. Immediately across the street from our house was the home of Eddie and Martha Peterson. Next door to the Petersons was the home of T. J. and Nancy French and their daughter Tina.

Elmer Arp was a retired postal carrier. In his retirement years, he did yard work. It kept him outside and healthy. When we moved into our house, we found from him, on our front porch, a basket of fruit. For almost twenty years, until the Arps moved to be nearer their daughter, Elmer cut our front grass, no charge. Carol used to say that if we ever sold this house, we would advertise that we had Elmer Arp for a neighbor. It would double the price. Carol said to Elmer, "I think I'll get rid of Cecil and run away with you." Elmer asked, "Is there a mortgage on your house?" Carol answered yes. Elmer rejoined, "I'm not running away with any woman with a mortgage."

Eddie Peterson was wheelchair bound. He had the worst case of rheumatoid arthritis I have ever seen. He was a very intelligent man. He could not do physical work, so he did mental work. He studied and invested in the stock market. When Martha died, some two years after Eddie's death, we learned how very successful he was. Martha left three and one-half million dollars to the Casey Eye Institute in Portland.

T. J. French was a retired Navy Chief. About two years after Carol and I moved to Portland, T. J. came to work for the same organization I did, the Army Corps of Engineers. He was one of the best thought-of employees with the Corps, except for one day each year, Army-Navy game day. He delighted in assuring our Division Commander, usually a two star General from West Point, that Navy would win.

Each day when I came home from work, I would see Eddie Peterson, sitting in front of his house. Before going inside our home, invariably, I would walk across the street and visit with him. That's how we met most of our neighbors. We all went to talk with Eddie. We called Eddie Peterson the "Mayor of Terwilliger."

One day I came home from work and found Carol reading a book, laughing, sometimes uncontained. I saw that the book is by John Steinbeck. I immediately asked myself, "What is the problem?" My wife is laughing while reading Steinbeck?

It was the book, *Travels with Charley*. In the book Steinbeck tells about a trip he took around the country accompanied by his dog, a poodle named Charley.

What did Carol like best about the book? She was tickled by what Steinbeck says about traveling through Fargo, North Dakota. Fargo, of course, is the home of North Dakota State University where she and I met, where we both went to college.

Steinbeck apparently anticipates the Fargo of legend, stagecoaches, cowboys, all that was the old west. The old west, he was really going to see. As he drives into Fargo, his legendary image is shattered. What he finds is a typical modern city,

tall buildings, department stores, cars, parking
meters, not what he wanted to see at all. As he
drives out of Fargo, his long held image is restored.
Fargo is again a rough city of the old west. This is
what Steinbeck has to say about Fargo, superfluous
words omitted:

> Curious how a place unvisited can take
> such hold on the mind that the very name sets
> up a ringing. To me such a place was Fargo,
> North Dakota. Perhaps its first impact is in the
> name Wells-Fargo, but my interest certainly
> goes beyond that. If you will take a map of the
> United States and fold it in the middle, eastern
> edge against western, and crease it sharply, right
> in the crease will be Fargo. I must admit that
> when I passed through Moorhead, Minnesota,
> and rattled across the Red River into Fargo on
> the other side, the countryside was no different
> from Minnesota over the river. I drove through
> the town as usual, seeing little but the truck
> ahead of me and the Thunderbird in my rear-
> view mirror. It's bad to have one's myth shaken
> up like that. As soon as I had cleared the
> outskirts I found with joy that the fact of Fargo
> had in no way disturbed my mind's picture of
> it. I could still think of Fargo as I always had --
> blizzard-riven, heat blasted, dust-raddled. I am
> happy to report that in the war between reality
> and romance, reality is not the stronger.

Carol chose to support our new community
as a volunteer. She served as an assistant
librarian with the Multnomah County Library,
and she worked with the Society of St. Vincent
de Paul, helping to feed, clothe, and house the
disadvantaged.

Oregon is in many respects a rain forest. Our
daughter Kris says, "When you live in Oregon, you
understand why there is more than one color green
in your paint box."

Anything planted in Oregon will grow, unless it is planted by me.

I planted some azaleas in our backyard. They all died. I said to Kris, "I don't understand. I know I come from a long line of farmers. You would think it would be bred into me; anything I plant should grow."

Kris responded, "Yes Dad, it's true you come from a long line of farmers. But there is no evidence that you come from a long line of successful farmers."

By nature, Freddie was a somewhat less than courageous dog.

Carol took him with her in the car to buy fertilizer from the garden shop. She parked her car. Men loaded the bags in the trunk. Freddie was very quiet. As Carol drove away, it was "Woof, woof, woof," as loud as can be. The garden shop workers were really told off, once his mother was back in the car, driving off, and all was safe.

If he thought he had to be, Fred could be a very courageous guard dog.

We were having storm windows installed. One of the workers crawled through an open window into the master bedroom. Carol was in the kitchen. Fred and Carol were home alone. Freddie positioned himself in the doorway between the bedroom and the hallway leading to the kitchen. He was barking, bouncing from side to side blocking the doorway. He was letting the man know that he would protect the woman he loved. His furor was saying, "You're not coming through here. You can't get to my mother." He was going to the mat. He would have let himself be killed to save Carol.

The trouble with dogs is that they get old. They get old too fast.

During our early years in Portland, when I came home from work, the moment he heard me at the door he would jump in circles, almost falling down the stairs to greet me, tail wagging. As he aged, he got to where he couldn't do it anymore. I always, first thing, walked over to greet him. Old age notwithstanding, his tail could still wag.

We took Fred to Dr. Ronald Shmidtke, a veterinarian well-respected in Oregon. Freddie needed an operation. Dr. Shmidtke said he didn't know what he'd find. He told us that if he found problems, real problems, he wasn't going to bring Freddie out.

Kris was in Chicago for some kind of convention. We called her to let her know that Fred was facing an operation and might not survive. She left Chicago early.

We were all so nervous that we made the dog nervous. The veterinarian said we had made the dog nervous. Fortunately, it didn't interfere with the operation.

The next time we feared death was when he first bloated up, suffered what veterinary medicine calls "Gastric Dilitation Volvuous," a swelling of the abdomen.

Late one evening, Fred had gone outside into our backyard. A long time passed, and he was not back. Carol and I went looking for him. We found him in a corner, under a bush. We saw his swollen body. We understood. It is instinctive for an old dog, when comes the hour of death, to leave the pack and die alone.

With Carol holding the dog as gently a possible, knowing that any touch was painful, and me driving, we rushed him to the Dove Lewis Emergency Animal Hospital. He was in the hospital overnight and most of the next day. When he saw Carol, he wagged his tail. The veterinary told us the cure was not permanent. We were thankful nonetheless. Dove Lewis had returned our dog to us, if only for a little while.

A few weeks later, we saw Freddie bloating again, this time inside the house. He moved closer to Carol and, with what little energy he had, wagged his swelling body one last time, as if saying to her, "I love you." We took him immediately to Dr. Shmidtke.

The veterinary told us there was nothing more he could do. The dog was going to die before morning. He recommended that we give our dog a shot, put him to sleep, to avoid suffering.

While Freddie was lying there, coming to the end, I was gently stroking him, careful not to cause pain. Carol was talking to him, saying what she knew he wanted to hear, "Nice boy, fine boy, good boy, my boy, I love you Freddie."

His was, I believe, the kindest death since that of St. Joseph, the husband of Mary.

That saintly man died with both Jesus the Christ and Mary the Mother of God at his bedside. Freddie died hearing the voice of the woman he loved, in the comforting presence of "parents" who loved him almost as if he were their child.

Fred was the one and only dog our family ever wanted.

A few days after Freddie died, we received in our mail a cherished card notifying us that "CONGREGATION B'NAI ISRAEL, Galveston, Texas, has received a contribution to its Vic Reiswerg fund from Leah and Charles Rosenbloom in memory of Fred Reinke."

Now some might say, "That's silly, you don't make a contribution commemorating the passing of a dog. After all, a dog is not a human." Others might think it facetious, some kind of a joke. Should any persons entertain these thoughts, they would be wrong. The Rosenblooms knew us, they knew our dog, and they knew the relationship we enjoyed together. Of course he was not a child. We would never suggest, or think, that losing him was the equivalent of losing a child. But we did love him. And the Rosenblooms well knew how much we loved him.

Someone I worked with in Galveston asked Mrs. Rosenbloom, "Did the Reinkes suffer a tragic loss in their family?" Leah answered, "Yes. They think they did."

twenty-one

Carol's children were not raised to participate in the sexual revolution. Carol had no difficulty explaining sex to her children. She said to me, "I have two kids and a dog. I'm not ashamed of how I got any one of them." Carol told Kris. Our older daughter asked, "Did Dad do that to you?" "Yes, of course," Carol confided, wanting the child to understand that it was all right. Afterwards, Carol said to me, "I could have sold you out." Years later Kris told me, "I thought she must have liked it, because she was too strong a woman to let you do it if she didn't."

She knew the proper response to the age old con, "If you loved me you would." Her answer, "If you loved me, you wouldn't ask."

My wife said two things about sex that I consider to be profound. "Sex is not a spectator sport." And, "The best sexual technique is love."

Not long after we moved to Portland, some idiot came up to our daughter during a social gathering and spouted, loud enough for others to hear, "Hey Kris, I hear you're a virgin." Kris stared at the oaf and answered in a voice strong enough for the same people to hear, "Don't worry about it. It's neither contagious nor incurable."

Later an acquaintance who Kris knew to be a lesbian sat beside her, "Kris, I see how you treat the boys. Could you perhaps be one of us?" Kris told her, "No. When I decide to engage in the sport, I'll play with the boys."

When Alison was twenty-one years old, she fell in love with a young man by the name of Courtney Lee Smith. My understanding is that Courtney asked if she would "come live with him." Alison said, "No, I won't do that. But I will marry you." Without a hint to us, they eloped. They were married on April 3, 1984. Now twenty-one years later, they are still married.

It was not a marriage to which Carol and I would then have consented. Alison was too young. We wanted her to stay in college, to first complete her education.

Our first grandchild was born four years later, on October 3, 1988.

While Alison was pregnant with their first child, she and Courtney decided on names. They told us, "If it's a boy, we'll call him Nicholas Lee. If it's a girl, we're going to name her Megan Leigh." Within moments after Alison gave birth, Courtney called our house. All he said was, "We got a Megan." Carol and I were in our car, heading for St. Vincent hospital. When we got there, we were in time to see the nurse cleaning our granddaughter. The child had red hair, beautiful red hair, the same dark, rich tone we saw those years ago on Alison. I heard Carol whisper under her breath, "Thank you God. You didn't let me see it the first time. Now you have."

I was less than happy with my son-in-law until after Megan was born. Once I saw how he treated his child, with far more patience than I showed my children, I wouldn't have traded him for any man on earth.

All births are special to mothers, but I believe the birth of Megan was extraordinarily special to our daughter. Alison was an adopted child. The birth of Megan presented the first time in her life that she knowingly had a biological relationship.

After Alison had Megan, she became acutely aware that she was the only member of our family who was not a college graduate. I don't think she wanted to tell this to Megan. She went back to college, taking mostly evening courses. She graduated from Concordia University on October 19, 1992, with a Bachelor of Science in Business Management and Communications.

I have always wondered why grandparents sometimes appear to have a favorite grandchild, the first. They don't. Certainly Carol didn't, and I don't. It's just that grandparents get to spend more time alone with a first grandchild. So they have more memories. From the time she was born until she was three, our oldest granddaughter Megan spent almost every Saturday with us. I called her "Megan Leigh P. B. Saturday Smith." The initials "P. B." stand for "perfect baby." Megan grew especially close to and trusting of her grandmother. Once when little Megan was ill, she said to her mother, "I don't feel good, I need to go to my grandmother's house to get care."

We saw more closely the growth of this first little granddaughter.

Megan learned to walk in our house. Our main living quarters, located on the second floor, has two fireplaces, back to back, one fronting the living room and one opening into the dining room. The walk around the fireplaces and a connecting wall is about sixty feet. Most kids learn to walk a few steps at a time, two steps, then three steps, before falling down into someone's arms. Not Megan. The first time she took more than two steps, she walked steadily for more than an hour. Fist clenched, face showing determination, she traversed this circle, again, and again, and again, and again.

We saw not only her abilities but also her confidence grow.

There was near our house a Burger King restaurant that housed a carrousel. Carol and I took Megan there almost every Saturday. At first she would not get onto the carrousel. All she could do was sit and watch. Then one day she said, "Papa, come with me." For several weeks she rode a horse with me standing beside her. The day came that she said to me, "Papa, you go sit down." That day, and all the days thereafter, she would ride the horse alone.

The Smith family, then only Alison, Courtney, and Megan, had a big, black cat. Once when Megan came to our house, we saw on her right hand a small cut. Megan explained, "When the cat bites you, you get an 'Owie.'"

When Megan was in the first grade, on the days she came to visit with us, she would want to play school. She, of course, would be the teacher. Carol and I would be her "pupils." If you want to know what goes on in your child's classroom, there is no better way to find out than playing school. You can hear every word the teacher says and the tone in which she says it. Megan ran a disciplined class, detailed assignments and no funny business. Carol said to me, after one of our sessions, "I thought we were both going to flunk."

Megan liked to pretend she worked in a bank. She would be a loan officer. I would be a customer seeking a loan. I said to her, "Honey, I'd like to borrow some money." I was immediately chastened, "Papa, you don't call your banker 'Honey.'"

In the second grade, Megan said to us, "I'm the second best reader in my class." Carol and I were very pleased. We both well knew that danger lurks if a child comes to expect that she must always be first. No one takes the blue ribbon for every life event.

Alison and Courtney have two other daughters, Emilee Anne, born on May 31, 1991, and Rachel Nicole, December 13, 1995. Emilee has red hair, the same dark, rich color we saw first on Alison and later on Megan. Rachel has brown hair like her father. I say to my youngest granddaughter, "You're the only little red-headed kid I've ever seen with brown hair."

Carol lauded Megan as "My best friend." She cherished Emilee as "My granddaughter." She acclaimed Rachel "My special gift." One day Megan said to her, "I'd like to be your special gift." Carol hugged and kissed our oldest granddaughter and said to her, "You are, Sweetheart. You really are!"

I say to each of Alison's children, "You're my best girl. You're my favorite granddaughter." They each know I say the same thing to the others, but they each like hearing it anyway.

My brother Norman says to his grandchildren, "There are ordinary kids, and there are 'Grand Kids.'" Norman's grandchildren believe it. Alison's children believe it.

When Emilee was three years old, she found a scissors and snipped off a chunk of her beautiful red hair. Her mother, Alison, asked her, "Why did you do that to your hair?" Emilee's response, "It was dirty."

I have a swatch of the hair she cut that day. To me it is treasure.

Emilee liked to play restaurant. She was the waitress. I was her patron. She would set the table in our dining room. I was allowed to enter only from the living room, never through the kitchen. She wrote out a menu, with prices. What I ordered, she would serve, maintaining proper etiquette. She always offered opportunity for dessert.

Both Emilee and Rachel played school in grandmother's house, with the same zeal shown earlier by Megan. I was their only pupil. Of course, they would never call a child in their class Papa. When we played school, I was given a name. I was always "John."

Rachel identified with the fact that, unlike her sisters, she had brown hair.

One day, while Alison was preparing dinner, four year old Rachel said to her mother, "I'm hungry, may I have a banana?" Alison answered, "No dear, we'll be eating very soon." Rachel turned to her father, "Dad, may I have a banana?" Courtney told her, "Your mother just said no, and what she says goes." Rachel protested. "I don't see why. She's an orange-head, and you're a brown-head. I think she should be in charge of the orange-heads, and you should be in charge of the brown-head."

Little girls like to play dress up. Alison's girls were no exception. Megan, Emilee, and Rachel in turn loved wearing their grandmother's wedding gown.

Alison and her family still live in Portland. Likely, Alison and Courtney will always live here. Courtney works at the Portland docks. He is a longshoreman.

Our daughter Kris now lives in Los Angeles. She operates her own pattern making business, part of the clothing industry. She is unmarried and may never marry. My wife said of this, "It's not the ark; we don't have to go through life two by two."

On the day she died, Carol was sixty-two years old. In exactly one more month she would have had her sixty-third birthday. I was sixty-three. We had been married forty years, six months and four days. I still keep her name on my checkbook. Both our names are still in the telephone book. She was, and always will be, "My wife."

Megan was eight years old. Emilee was five. Rachel was not yet two.

When Carol died, we all suffered. I think Megan suffered the most.

twenty-two

Carol was always a healthy woman. When she was in grade school, she had her appendix removed. Other than that, until her final illness, she was never hospitalized.

Almost every Sunday during the last fifteen years of her life, Carol and I went to breakfast after church with four friends, Robert and Yvonne Polich, and Glenn and Anna Pringle. Bob Polich was a retired school teacher. Glenn Pringle owned a restaurant.

One Sunday, while we were enjoying our meal, Carol felt a sudden, sharp pain in her back, as if a bone had broken. She told me about it on our way home.

Within a few days, Carol was started on a series of medical tests. It was determined that she had cancer. An operation, expected to be successful, was scheduled.

The operation over, the surgeon came to see me. He had removed the cancer, but it had metastasized, spread to the liver. The tumor in the liver was located where it was inoperable. It could not be removed without causing her death.

The surgeon said he would ask a priest to come see me. I did not want to see a priest. To a priest was not where I would go for comfort. While Carol was in the recovery room, I drove to my daughter Alison's house. My granddaughter Emilee was home. I hugged the little darling, tears flowing. When I was allowed to see Carol, I was there. She took one look at me and knew that all had not gone well.

We were scheduled to see an oncologist. Oncology is a word I did not know and wish I had never learned. The oncologist was Dr. Eldon Andersen. Dr. Andersen was kind, but candid. He told Carol she had a choice. If she elected to undergo chemotherapy she would live for another eighteen months. If she elected to forgo chemotherapy, she would die in about three months.

We elected to submit to the difficulties associated with chemotherapy.

Carol tried to make things easier for Dr. Andersen, to inject a little levity into her situation. She well understood that there is nothing harder on a doctor than being unable to cure a patient. One time he prescribed for her some calcium pills. "Isn't this nice," she said to me, for benefit of the oncologist, "he doesn't want me to develop osteoporosis."

We flew to Mesa, Arizona, where Grace Roehrich was living with Carol's brother Jim. Carol knew she would have to tell her mother. Carol's mother hugged her daughter. She would be strong, she would be supportive, she would not cry. That night the woman called her son Bob in Richmond, Texas. Bob could hardly hear for his mother crying.

Thankfully, we thought, Nicholas J. Roehrich did not have to hear this. He had died five years earlier, on August 7, 1990. Carol's mother would outlive her daughter by thirteen months. She died on April 24, 1998.

Carol told me something every world leader should be required to hear.

While her family lived in Langdon, Carol's parents owned a Fairway grocery store. Adjacent to the Roehrich grocery was a business owned by the Boyd family, the Golden Rule Department Store. During World War II, in 1943, the Boyd's son Jimmy was killed. Jimmy Boyd was a Navy pilot, flying off a carrier. Hearing this news, Carol's parents visited with the Boyd family, offering condolence. They took Carol and her little brother Ronnie with them. Carol was nine years old. Ronnie was almost two. Carol remembered holding Ronnie by his hand, silently knowing she was in the presence of adults in deep sorrow. She said to me, "None of us could have imagined, on that day, that the same fate awaited this little boy."

I hear Peter, Paul and Mary and the Kingston Trio, "Where Have All the Flowers Gone?" I ask, having lived with her pain, "When will they ever learn?"

Carol planned our fortieth wedding celebration. It was a catered affair with some sixty guests. It was held in our home on Saturday, September 21, 1996. Carol's mother and her brother Jim came from Mesa, Arizona. Her brother Bob and his wife Shinta flew in from Richmond, Texas. My brother Walter and his wife Dorothy came from Helena, Montana. My brother Ruben attended from Idaho Falls, Idaho. His wife Marlys had died fourteen years earlier. My brother Norman and his wife Helen traveled from Charles Town, West Virginia. An especially welcome guest was Pat Liebler Pearson. Carol and Pat met in the first grade in Langdon, North Dakota. They had been close friends ever since. Pat and her husband Paul flew in from Woodside, California.

It was the last time our home would be overflowing with friends.

While Carol was sick, I thought back to a conversation I had with David Nelson, one of the lawyers already working in my office when I became the Division Counsel.

I found, when I arrived in Portland, an attorney employed in the Office of Counsel who was not interested in working. I will call him Billy

Tryer. He was, in his mind, a trial lawyer, and only a trial lawyer. He had no case being tried, and no prospect of future cases to try. In the Federal courts, the Corps is represented by attorneys from the Department of Justice. The only cases tried by Corps lawyers are those before the Corps of Engineers Board of Contract Appeals and the Armed Services Board of Contract Appeals. At this time, all cases before the Boards were tried by lawyers working in the districts.

My predecessor, a fine lawyer but an indulgent manager, had made a deal with him. The deal was this. This "trial lawyer" would be promoted and made the Deputy Division Counsel, on condition that he would do other legal work, not just trial work. Until his promotion came through, Mr. Tryer lived up to the deal. As soon as promoted, he went back to being only a "trial lawyer." Again, he would do nothing else.

I asked him for a list of all the cases he had tried during the past five years. The list was short, only four cases. My thought was that I could hire Melvin Belli cheaper. I decided to abolish his job. He would no longer be retired on duty at Government expense.

David Nelson came in to see me. He said, "Mr. Reinke, you don't have to get rid of Billy. You can supervise him. You can make him work."

I told David, "You're right, I could supervise him. I could make him work. But I do not surround myself with people who will work only when I am watching them. I want people who will work when I can't watch them. People I can count on when I am not at my best, lawyers who will support me when I am at my weakest."

While Carol was coping with cancer, I was at my weakest. I will be forever grateful that I had strong support from the lawyers in my office. Rebecca B. Ransom, John R. Seeronen, Gayle N. Lear, and David G. Nelson carried the load.

Carol was a very religious woman, with a strong belief in God. She went to church and took me and our children to church every Sunday. She considered the relationship between a person and his or her God to be a very personal relationship. She said to me, "Asking people about their relationship with God is to me a more offensive invasion of privacy than asking them about their sex life." She did not believe there is any one "right" religion for all people. She believed there was one right religion for each person.

"I pray," she said, "but I never ask God to cure me. That is not something I think I should do. I ask God to help me to get through this. That I know He will do."

I saw how this good woman got through her ordeal. She spent her last months preparing her children, and her husband, to continue life without her. She made special financial arrangements for our children. She hired a woman to clean our house. She taught me to cook my favorite dishes. She stayed in charge until the day she died.

She died at 4:56 in the morning, on Wednesday, March 26, 1997. Kris and I were with her, watching over her, when she died. The moment before, she leaned forward from the waist, sat straight up, arms extended, on her face the most glorious smile I have ever seen. Some people would think that this Christian woman was seeing Jesus Christ. I do not. Jesus Christ is a God too generous and loving to have dominated Carol's first glimpse of heaven. What I believe Carol saw was her little brother Ronnie running across a spring field of green being chased by a little poodle named Fred.

I worked for the United States Army one more year after Carol died, forty years in all. Dwight David Eisenhower was president when I started. William Jefferson Clinton was in office when I retired on June 3, 1998. Upon my retirement I received a letter from President Clinton, routine, but nonetheless appreciated. The letter reads:

Mr. Cecil E. Reinke
7805 Southwest Terwilliger
Portland, Oregon 97219

Dear Cecil:

Congratulations on your retirement from
the Department of the Army.

America's tradition of hard work has
made us strong, and you can be proud of your
contribution to that legacy. Your dedication to
the public is an inspiration to others. On behalf
of all those who have benefited from your
service, I thank you for a job well done.

Hillary and I wish you good health and
every future success.

Sincerely,

Bill Clinton

I still live in the house we bought on
Terwilliger Boulevard. In this house I see every
day things that remind me of Carol. I walk on
carpet she had installed. I use appliances she
selected. I draw curtains she made. I don't expect
to move.

I wanted Carol with me in my old age. I am in
my old age. She is with me.

Printed in the United States
By Bookmasters